THUCYDIDES
AND THE
SCIENCE OF HISTORY

THUCYDIDES
AND THE SCIENCE
OF HISTORY

By

CHARLES NORRIS COCHRANE

NEW YORK

RUSSELL & RUSSELL · INC

1965

FIRST PUBLISHED IN 1929
REISSUED, 1965, BY RUSSELL & RUSSELL, INC.
L. C. CATALOG CARD NO: 65-17885
PRINTED IN THE UNITED STATES OF AMERICA

TO

WILLIAM STAFFORD MILNER

CONTENTS

I

INTRODUCTION

CRITICS of Thucydides have been almost unanimous in associating him with the period of enlightenment of the fifth century B.C. With one notable exception,[1] the English commentators have agreed that the *Histories* reflect not a 'mythological conception of the world of human acts and passions . . . derived from an early education consisting almost exclusively in the study of the poets',[2] but rather the rationalist and humanist atmosphere of the days of Anaxagoras and Protagoras.

In one respect, however, Cornford and his critics appear to be in agreement. 'The want of scientific categories, and above all of the cardinal conception of law as applying to human actions, makes a gulf between Thucydides and ourselves immensely greater than any which his want of superstitious beliefs makes between him and Herodotus.' This statement of Cornford (p. 74) finds a parallel in the judgement of Bury[3] that 'with the Greeks, historical study never acquired the scientific character which it was reserved for the nineteenth century to impress upon it'. Shotwell, in his article on Thucydides in the *History of History*, develops this criticism at greater length, complaining that Thucydides like all the ancients neglected the economic and social forces upon which modern scientific history lays so much stress. Grundy,[4] indeed, ascribes to Thucydides belief in a theory of cycles, as a means of accounting for the fact that history repeats itself, and of justifying his claim that his work is useful and a 'possession for ever'. A theory of cycles, however, is no more scientific than a theory of progress or of declension from a golden age, and, indeed, the metaphysical implications of such a view are clearly apparent from the use which Plato makes of it in his pseudo-historical account of the evolution of Greek civilization (*Laws*, iii).

[1] F. M. Cornford, *Thucydides Mythistoricus*.
[2] Op. cit., p. ix.   [3] *Ancient Greek Historians*, p. 147.
[4] *Thucydides and the History of his Age*, p. 8.

Gomperz, while denying by implication that Thucydides was affected by any metaphysical presuppositions, nevertheless supports the charge that he possessed no scientific categories to replace them. 'In so far, then', he says,[1] 'the sympathies of Thucydides tended to the physicists and the meteorologists. But we can scarcely assume that he was satisfied for any length of time with either of the attempts then hanging in the balance to solve the great riddle of the universe, whether with that of Leucippus or with that of Anaxagoras. His repugnance to both would probably have been due not so much to their divergence from the tenets of popular religion as to their intrinsic boldness and undemonstrableness.'

But scepticism in regard to the whole is not incompatible with a firm belief in the value of inquiries into the parts. Philosophy may continue her vain attempt to storm the bastions of heaven; but positive science, like warfare, proceeds by the method of limited objectives; and indeed often scores her greatest advances at those moments in human history when religious and philosophic doubt are most acute. In the case of Thucydides, it would seem clear that, while the sceptical rationalism of his age accounts sufficiently for his critical attitude regarding the phenomena of nature, something akin to the positive faith of the modern scientist is needed to explain the note of calm assurance with which he commends his *Histories* to the world as a possession for ever. Whatever else may be questionable, it is perfectly evident that he has no doubt of the value and usefulness of his own work.

This self-assurance has often been noticed as a characteristic of Thucydides; and has been ascribed partly to the literary convention existing among ancient historians, that each should pose as in some way superior to his predecessors, and partly also to the lack of that modesty (or mock-modesty) which is supposed to be a product of modern times. It is the purpose of this essay to maintain that at least in Thucydides, there is another explanation than that of mere vanity, or literary good form; and at the same time to suggest an hypothesis better calculated to explain this and other characteristic features of

[1] *Greek Thinkers*, i. 512.

his work than any which has come to the attention of the writer.

The truth is that Thucydides had the assured faith of a scientist because he was a scientist, because, in fact, he was inspired by contact with a department of positive science which in his day had succeeded in extricating itself from the coils of cosmology, and which by means of a method adequate to the most rigid modern demands was already advancing to conclusions which were recognized as valid and immensely significant for human life. From the remarks of Plato it may be inferred that mathematics had in his day reached this point, and was esteemed by some of the Sophists at least by reason of its practical value, but mathematics has at best a remote connexion with human life. On the other hand, biological and medical science deals directly with humanity in its normal and pathological conditions. And, in the second half of the fifth century, biology and medicine were already established as fruitful sciences in the hands of the Hippocratic school. The intellectual and spiritual affiliations of Thucydides were with this school. The general philosophic background, so far as this is discernible, is the thought of Democritus rather than of Anaxagoras, his alleged tutor. Specifically, however, his inspiration comes from Hippocrates, along with the principles of method which determined the character of his work. The *Histories* of Thucydides represent an attempt to apply to the study of social life the methods which Hippocrates employed in the art of healing, and constitute an exact parallel to the attempts of modern scientific historians to apply evolutionary canons of interpretation derived from Darwinian science.

II

THE BACKGROUND

Influence of the Atomistic Philosophy

'I CAME to Athens, and nobody knew me!' Thus did Democritus give expression to the surprise and indignation which he felt at his reception in Athens, when he visited the imperial city. He had cause to be annoyed, but should not have been astonished, that the Athenians were ignorant both of his name and of his work. The Athens which he visited was the Athens of Anaxagoras and Pericles, and in such an atmosphere there was no possible welcome for the man who had deposed the fashionable νοῦς from its position at the head of the cosmos, and explained the γένεσις and φθορά of all phenomenal things as the result of a fortuitous concourse of atoms moving according to the law of their own nature. Yet at Abdera, it is said, the name of Democritus was one to conjure with, and the very characteristics of his thought which made him *persona non grata* in Athens supplied a congenial background for the ideas of what one may perhaps, without being too fanciful, characterize as the School of Abdera, a school to which Thucydides the sociologist, no less than Hippocrates the physician, probably belonged.

The principles of the atomists which affected the physician and the sociologist, so far as these were affected by philosophic principles, may be briefly summarized as follows. First in importance was the doctrine of causality, *ex nihilo nihil fit*, formulated by Leucippus and adopted by his successor. It is superfluous to explain that the uniformity of nature is presupposed by all positive science. To Hippocrates and Thucydides therefore this doctrine was of fundamental importance, and Gomperz[1] points out that Anaxagoras was at that very moment obscuring the solution of the problem of nature by dragging in a factor approximating to God. But Democritean

[1] Whitehead, *Science and the Modern World*, pp. 223, 319.

theory pointed to a world which was explicable without reference to extraneous conceptions such as the νοῦς of Anaxagoras, or the Empedoclean 'Love and Strife', no less than to the naïve personifications of popular religion current in Aeschylean tragedy—a world moreover in which τύχη reigned supreme, and from which final causes were rigidly excluded.

The 'atmosphere' of philosophic thought is no less significant than its positive achievements. It is generally admitted, for instance, that the atmosphere of Platonism has at all times been unfavourable to positive science, because of its insistence upon the exclusive significance of the abstract universals of thought, as opposed to the concrete particulars of the phenomenal world. In the fifth century there were powerful influences abroad analogous to Platonism, such as the doctrines of the Eleatic school, which either imposed an effective barrier to all thought about mundane things, or at any rate diverted thought to by-paths such as grammar and rhetoric.   The exact reverse, however, was true of the speculation of the atomist school, which was dominated by the keenest respect for the world of γένεσις and φθορά, and which aimed at all costs to 'save the appearances'. Such an atmosphere is vital to the life of the human sciences, whether biological or social.

The phenomenal world, according to the atomists, is to be apprehended by experience, and in no other way; but to emphasize the significance of experience is to emphasize the significance of history, which is nothing more or less than the record of human experience in relation to the external world.

Without entering upon the vexed question of the quality of the experience in relation to the 'outside' world, one may conclude by reminding the reader that 'the atomists', to quote the words of Gomperz,[1] 'were, in common with the rest of their predecessors and contemporaries in natural philosophy, with the sole exception of Anaxagoras, materialists inasmuch as they looked for the only causes or conditions of the states and qualities of consciousness in the material world alone'. This is not to say that they excluded from their purview the concept of mind. It remained for twentieth-century America

[1] *Greek Thinkers*, i. 355.

to discover and designate 'behaviourism'. All that is implied of the atomists is the limitation of knowledge to scientific analysis, and the doctrine that all psychical processes bear an ordered, and therefore ascertainable, relationship to their respective stimuli; or, in other words, are relative to the circumstances that provoke them.

Enough has been said to suggest that the atomistic philosophy of the fifth century B.C. was not merely congenial to, but the necessary preliminary of, the growth of the special sciences of human behaviour. The question remains: to what extent did the speculations of the atomists actually serve to stimulate the beginnings of these sciences? Democritus himself may be said to have initiated scientific (as opposed to philosophic) research; the records of his voluminous writings noted by Diogenes Laertius (following the general treatment of nature, the περὶ φύσιος πρῶτον) are:

1. Human Nature, or The Flesh, περὶ ἀνθρώπου φύσιος (ἢ περὶ σαρκός) δεύτερον.

2.⎫
3.⎭ Psychology $\left\{\begin{matrix} περὶ νοῦ \\ περὶ αἰσθησίων \end{matrix}\right\}$ = περὶ ψυχῆς.

4. Flavours, περὶ χυμῶν.

5. Colours, περὶ χροῶν.

6. Variety of Shapes, περὶ τῶν διαφερόντων ῥυσμῶν.

7. Images (or Prediction), περὶ εἰδώλων (ἢ περὶ προνοίας).

—the very names of which suggest the scope and nature of his interests. There follow several special studies of causation in different types of phenomena, physical as in the case of celestial phenomena or of magnetism, psychical as in the case of sounds, &c.

But for the purposes of the present inquiry the most important are included in the so-called technical treatises, which comprise works on medicine, viz.:

Descriptive Analysis (πρόγνωσις), Diet (περὶ διαίτης ἢ διατη-τικόν), the Science of Medicine (ἰητρικὴ γνώμη), and the miscellaneous works quoted by Diogenes at the end of his list, especially Fever (περὶ πυρετοῦ), Coughs arising from illness (τῶν ἀπὸ νόσου βησσόντων), and Scientific Research (περὶ ἱστορίης).

Influence of the Hippocratic School of Physicians

Tradition points very strongly to a close association between Democritus and the Father of Medicine. But, apart from the anecdotes recounted by Diogenes Laertius, and from the epistles included in the Hippocratic corpus, there is an intrinsic probability that Hippocrates made the acquaintance of Democritus during his years of practice at Abdera and the neighbouring island of Thasos. This probability is confirmed by the close correspondence between their respective points of view.

Hippocrates was, of course, a practical man, engaged first and foremost in the art of healing. Accordingly, it is vain to look in his works for any explicit discussion of the purely theoretical topics which came within the purview of the Father of Physics, whom Aristotle described as 'the great Democritus', and of whom he remarked that 'no one before him had dealt with growth and change except in the most superficial way— and he seems to have thought of everything'. Yet, without the confidence inspired by an acquaintance with Democritean logic and physics, how could Hippocrates have proceeded to delimit the scope of biological and medical science, detaching it on the one hand from religion and philosophy, and on the other raising it from a condition of mere empiricism and quackery to the assured status of positive science? This, however, was the task essayed by the author of *Ancient Medicine*, whom the critics agree in regarding as a fifth-century representative of the Hippocratic school, if not indeed Hippocrates himself.

The treatise, *Ancient Medicine*, stands out for all time as the first clear statement of the principles of rational empiricism. Medicine had existed as an empirical art from the days of Homer; and, through the activity of the Cnidian school in describing and 'tagging' diseases, had come within measurable distance of being a science. Empedocles, however, and the philosophers generally had attempted to bind medicine to the cart-wheel of philosophy. This, says the author of the treatise, is their fundamental error. The riddle of the universe may remain unsolved; and yet physical science both can and ought to progress independently. 'I consider that in regard to natural

science clear knowledge is derived from no other source whatsoever than from medical science. The knowledge of nature
can be grasped, if and when one properly comprehends the
science of medicine, but until then, it is in my opinion utterly
impossible. It is this field of research which I claim for my own;
viz. the nature of man and an accurate knowledge of causation
in this field' (ch. xx).

On the other hand, the defect of primitive medicine was apparent. Hit or miss empiricism had carried it a goodly distance,
as, for instance, in the knowledge of diet.[1] It stopped short,
however, of classification (τὸ εἶδος) and of penetrating by induction (γνώμη) to the principle (λόγος) of health and disease.
The knowledge so acquired is doubtless relative, but none the
less 'useful' on that account. For instance, it enables the physician to forecast, and it is an excellent thing for the physician
to practise forecasting.[2] The ability to *predict* is thus laid down
as the essence of science.

How is such prediction possible? By experience and experience alone. 'If a man intends to predict with assurance
(προγιγνώσκειν) who will survive, who will succumb, and who
will be subject to the disease for a longer time and who for
a shorter, he must first familiarize himself completely with all
the symptoms[3] (τὰ σημεῖα ἐκμανθάνοντα πάντα). He will then be
in a position to judge, estimating their relative importance.
He must have a clear appreciation of the symptoms and other
indications (εἰδέναι περὶ τῶν τεκμηρίων καὶ τῶν ἄλλων σημείων),
because at all times and places bad symptoms have the same
bad significance and good symptoms the reverse. In Africa,
Greece, and Scythia, it is evident that the symptoms which
have been previously noted give truthful indications. He must
therefore realize that in the same localities it is not surprising
if he usually hits upon the right diagnosis (τὰ πολλαπλάσια
ἐπιτυγχάνειν) provided that he knows how to judge and
estimate them aright. All the diseases that reach a climax at

---

[1] Ch. iii ἄλλα τε πολλὰ περὶ ταῦτα πρηγματευσάμενοι [experimenting] ἤψησάν
τε καὶ ὤπτησαν καὶ ἔμιξαν καὶ ἐκέρασαν τὰ ἰσχυρά τε καὶ ἄκρητα τοῖς ἀσθενεστέροις,
πλάσσοντες πάντα πρὸς τὴν ἀνθρώπου φύσιν τε καὶ δύναμιν.

[2] *Prognostic*, i. τὸν ἰητρὸν δοκεῖ μοι ἄριστον εἶναι πρόνοιαν ἐπιτηδεύειν.

[3] Ib. xxv.

the aforesaid times may be recognized by the same symptoms (γνώσῃ τοῖσιν αὐτοῖσι σημείοισιν).'

This important passage has been quoted in full because it illustrates so beautifully the specific qualities of Hippocratic science. There are, he says, certain uniformities of pathological condition, and these may be ascertained by the competent observer. But such uniformities are ascertainable only by close attention to the symptoms. In other words, the possibility of prediction depends on close attention to facts (the ἔργα of Thucydides), coupled with intelligent appreciation of the significance of the facts (the Thucydidean λόγοι); and this, in short, is science.

But what applies to pathological applies equally to normal conditions. In the treatise, *Airs, Waters, Places* (well described as the first exposition of the fundamental principles of public health), the author examines at length normal as well as abnormal conditions of human beings in relation to their environment, with a view to forecasting what will *probably* happen when changes in the environment occur.[1] In this treatise also, the factors to be considered are but two, viz. (1) a human nature (ἡ ἀνθρωπεία φύσις) relatively stable but possessing various potentialities (δυνάμιες), and (2) the environmental conditions, differing according to geography, but in each district relatively uniform from year to year. It is further assumed that the physical environment determines in general not merely the bodily characteristics of the inhabitants but their mental characteristics as well. Thus, speaking of Asiatics, he says the inhabitants are well nourished, of great beauty of appearance, and of immense size and, furthermore, uniform in their beauty and size. Asia is tamer than Europe and the inhabitants are characteristically milder and more good tempered.[2] On the other hand, the bravery, endurance, industry, and high spirit of Europeans are accounted for in just the same way.

Questions of profound interest and importance for science

[1] Ch. xi κατὰ ταὐτά τις ἐννοεύμενος καὶ σκοπεύμενος προειδείη ἂν τὰ πλεῖστα τῶν μελλόντων ἔσεσθαι ἀπὸ τῶν μεταβολέων.
[2] Ch. xii ἥ τε χώρη τῆς χώρης ἡμερωτέρη καὶ τὰ ἤθεα τῶν ἀνθρώπων ἠπιώτερα καὶ εὐοργητότερα.

are raised, if not settled, in the same treatise. Thus, in connexion with the so-called Long-heads, there is raised the
question of heredity[1] and environment, in which the clichés of
contemporary speculation are employed in perhaps a fresh and
more significant sense. 'Originally custom (i. e. the custom of
binding the head) was chiefly responsible for the length of the
head, but now nature also comes to the assistance of custom.'[2]
Here it is asserted that there is inherent in custom (the external)
an element of compulsion, while nature (the integral) acts with
spontaneity. The passage also emphasizes the significance and
reality of the time factor in transforming the customary into
the natural.

The word *nomos* has been translated 'custom', but, as may
be seen from a subsequent passage, it carries an immensely
richer significance than the English word. As employed in the
treatise, it really means the habit that is induced by the necessity
of conforming to conditions, and so equals the whole institutional environment, which is here given its due importance.[3]
Geographical environment comes first, as the stage-setting of
human life. But the institutional environment with which men
surround themselves is no less significant, and, while in the
main it cannot but correspond to external conditions, it nevertheless admits of and indeed includes that kind of motivation
which we consider psychical.[4] Apart from the effects of climate
and soil, so runs the argument, the Asiatics as a rule are un-
manly because they are unwilling to risk their lives and fortunes
on behalf of their despotic kings; while those few inhabitants
of Asia, whether Greek or non-Greek, who are not ruled by
despots, but are independent, toiling for their own advantage,
are exceptionally warlike. On the other hand, the aggressive

---

[1] Heredity is also discussed in chapter v of the *Sacred Disease*, and there
made responsible for all diseases.

[2] Ch. xiv τὴν μὲν ἀρχὴν ὁ νόμος αἰτιώτατος ἐγένετο τοῦ μήκεος τῆς κεφαλῆς, νῦν
δὲ καὶ ἡ φύσις συμβάλλεται τῷ νόμῳ. The discussion continues οὕτως τὴν ἀρχὴν
ὁ νόμος κατειργάσατο, ὥστε ὑπὸ βίης τοιαύτην τὴν φύσιν γενέσθαι· τοῦ δὲ χρόνου
προϊόντος ἐν φύσει ἐγένετο, ὥστε τὸν νόμον μηκέτι ἀναγκάζειν.

[3] Ch. xvi εἴ τις φύσει πέφυκεν ἀνδρεῖος καὶ εὔψυχος ⟨ἀνάγκη⟩ ἀποτρέπεσθαι τὴν
γνώμην ὑπὸ τῶν νόμων.

[4] Ch. xvi διὰ ταύτας ἐμοὶ δοκεῖ τὰς προφάσιας ἀναλκὲς εἶναι τὸ γένος τὸ Ἀσιηνὸν
καὶ προσέτι διὰ τοὺς νόμους.

and independent disposition of Europeans is due not only to
the greater variety of geographical conditions prevalent in
Europe, but also to the political and social environment that
has evolved in correspondence with those conditions.[1]

A further observation of great significance occurs in the same
passage, namely, that change (or, as we should say, evolution)
is the result of shock, which rouses the temper of man and
prevents its stagnation. Accordingly, there is no progress
possible in the uniform conditions of Asiatic life, except,
perhaps, such as may be brought about by contacts with the
more aggressive peoples who are produced in other climes.
For in Asia nothing occurs to occasion violent mental shocks
(ἐκπλήξιες τῆς γνώμης) or bodily disturbances, and yet these
shocks are more likely to inflame the temper and impart to it an
element of brute courage than is an unvaried monotony. Thus
both the classical notion that degeneracy, and the modern
notion that progress develops as the result of purely internal
and spontaneous changes of the human spirit, are rigidly
excluded.

This great generalization put the Hippocratics in a position
to criticize current notions of causation in the field of human
activity, and in particular those derived from the popular
religion. As an example of such criticism may be cited the
passage[2] in which the author discusses the prevalence of impotence among males of Scythia. The natives, he says, attribute the cause of this impotence to God (τὴν αἰτίην προστιθέασι
θεῷ), and worship the wretched victims, each fearing for himself.
'In my opinion also these afflictions are divine, and all others
likewise. There is none of them which is more divine or more
human than another, but all are alike and all divine. Each
one of them has its own nature and none occurs except naturally
(οὐδὲν ἄνευ φύσιος γίνεται).' Proceeding, he attributes the cause
of this particular affliction to Scythian habits of life in the saddle
(ἡ τοιαύτη νοῦσος ἀπὸ τοιαύτης προφάσιος τοῖς Σκύθῃσι γίνεται
οἵην εἴρηκα). The discussion also throws light on a characteristic
feature of Greek theology, common to Roman theology as well,

---

[1] Ch. xxiii, ad fin. οὕτως οἱ νόμοι οὐχ ἥκιστα τὴν εὐψυχίην ἐργάζονται.
[2] Airs, Waters, Places, xxii.

namely, that the gods are thought of as responsive to prayers, supplications, and gifts, and expected to return the favours which their worshippers bestow upon them, in the concrete forms of health, wealth, and happiness. We are not concerned to bring out the shallowness of this notion, although one is irresistibly reminded by contrast of the cry of the Hebrew: 'Though he slay me, yet will I trust him.' But the author notes the vanity of the attempt to buy the favour of heaven, and, in this, as in other passages, takes religious feeling into account, but only as a subjective manifestation of the human spirit. From the standpoint of science, this is all that he or any one is entitled to do.

The subject of divine intervention in human affairs is renewed in the treatise on the *Sacred Disease* or epilepsy, which the superstitious Romans, for reasons that are familiar, spoke of as *morbus comitialis*. This treatise may be, as some think, a thesis set by the master to a pupil on the theme of 'Superstition and Medicine'. At any rate, the seizures which popular thought ascribed to possession by a god or a devil are therein referred, like the Scythian disease, to natural causes alone, and a vigorous and ironical attack is launched against the unscientific dualism which accounted for some such phenomena as 'natural', while referring others to the 'divine'. In chapter iv may be noted the attitude of genuine Greek science towards purifications ($\kappa\alpha\theta\alpha\rho$-$\mu o\iota$). These are examined in a spirit which, though it might have appealed to Thucydides, would hardly have done so even to Plato. Chapter xv describes the mental reaction of the victims, in the same spirit though not with the same vividness of detail as Thucydides employs in his account of the conduct of those who suffered from the plague.

One more consideration will complete, for present purposes, the analysis of Hippocratic thought. Throughout, it has been assumed that scientific knowledge is relative, and that the 'absolute' truths of philosophy have nothing to do with science. It follows from this that successful prediction is possible only in the main and generally;[1] or, in other words, that scientific penetration ($\gamma\nu\omega\mu\eta$) yields nothing more than probability

[1] $\pi o\lambda\lambda\alpha\pi\lambda\alpha\sigma\iota\omega s$ and $\dot{\omega}s$ $\dot{\epsilon}\pi\grave{\iota}$ $\tau\grave{\alpha}$ $\pi\lambda\epsilon\hat{\iota}\sigma\tau\alpha$ as in the sentences quoted above.

(τὸ εἰκός). 'Chance' or 'Fortune' therefore is depersonalized and, at the same time, the word (τύχη) is emptied of metaphysical significance. The term is used to describe that which does not yield to scientific analysis, or simply the incalculable element in human affairs.

III

THUCYDIDES

IDEAS such as those enunciated by the Hippocratic school were unquestionably floating about in the Hellenic world as early as the middle of the fifth century B.C. Herodotus, for example, was well aware of the requirements of a genuinely scientific hypothesis, as he showed by his refusal to accept the theory of a 'stream of ocean', or any other figment of the poetic imagination, as an adequate explanation of the periodic rise and fall of the waters of the Nile. He also displayed familiarity with the theory that physical conditions determine human character, when he remarked, in his concluding chapter, as though to point the moral of his history, that 'soft countries are wont to produce soft inhabitants. It is impossible that the same land should yield an excellent harvest and men who are good in war'. Now if Herodotus had consistently made use of these principles as canons of historical interpretation, instead of introducing the religious or metaphysical principles which he actually employed, he might still have produced a great work, but it would have been an anticipation of Thucydides rather than the work which we actually possess. As it was, he frequently employed scientific standards both in the examination of fact (τὸ ἔργον) and in its interpretation (ὁ λόγος). The interpretation, for instance, of the Persian defeat at Plataea (ix. 62) as being the result of inferiority not in brains or strength, but in equipment and in the science of warfare, is quite 'scientific'. But it is when Herodotus comes to the ultimate questions of human history that he reaches an impasse; the reason being that he is unable to determine whether it is ultimately God or man who pulls the strings. This difficulty is illustrated by the passage (vii. 1–19) in which he discusses the causes of the Persian invasion. The physical causes having been expounded with great vigour and perspicacity, he finally turns from them as inadequate, and imports God in the shape of a nocturnal vision, to account for the act which Thucydides would have unquestionably referred to the love of domination and the prospect of power. If then, in the judgement of moderns, Herodotus is inferior to Thucydides, it is not because he is a 'romancer'. That theory should long ago have been discarded. If we praise Thucydides and decry Herodotus at the present day, it is because our spiritual affiliations are with 'science' rather than with 'philosophy'; for Thucydides is the most scientific, as Herodotus is the most philosophic of Greek historians.

It has been thought necessary to depict at some length the background of Thucydides' thought for two reasons. Firstly, Cornford, in his brilliant and powerful argument, has referred the *Histories* to quite another setting. Secondly, the critics of Cornford, while they have put their fingers on what are without doubt the genuine characteristics of Thucydides, do not seem to have accounted adequately for the fact that those characteristics emerge in his work. Thus, in their hands, Thucydides himself appears as a portent, an 'uncaused' phenomenon in the stream of European thought. Bury, for instance, speaks of his 'powerful and original mind'; and a recent writer[1] says: 'It is all the more to the credit of Thucydides that, living in an age when scientists still occupied themselves with problems altogether beyond the reach of scientific investigation, he did not allow his mind to wander into barren speculations, but kept it with unswerving steadfastness to those lines of thought upon which experience or deduction from experience could be brought to bear profitably. Upon these lines he concentrates his whole attention; and for the rest he has nothing to do but to take the universe as he finds it.' These critics go too far. In the fifth century B.C., at least in the one department of medicine, genuine science had emerged among the Greeks; and the power and originality of Thucydides lies in his having attempted to adapt the principles and methods of that science to the study of society.

There is no doubt that Thucydides, through his well-known connexion with the Thrace-ward regions, had at least the opportunity of meeting the Father of Medicine and becoming familiar

[1] G. F. Abbott, *Thucydides, A Study in Historical Reality*, Routledge, 1925, p. 76.

with his work. That he actually did so is a probable inference from the close and, in some cases, startling analogies of style between the *Histories* and the *Corpus Hippocraticum*. These analogies have been noticed by most thoughtful students. Forbes, for instance, in his introduction to Thucydides i, recalls the penetrating observation of Littré:[1] 'Thucydides lived and wrote at the same time as the physician of Cos; the more I have reflected on the style of the two, and sought to penetrate into its processes, its form, and its feeling, the more fully I am convinced that a close affinity existed between these writers. . . . It is to Thucydides that Hippocrates must be compared; in both we have a grave way of speaking, a style full of vigour, a choice of phrases full of meaning, and a use of the Greek language, which, although great pains have been taken with it, is nevertheless less flowing than that of Plato.' He then cites the *Airs, Waters, Places* (ch. xvi) as exhibiting these analogies of style.

It is our contention, however, that the analogy goes much deeper than mere style: that, in fact, Thucydides adapted the principles and methods of Hippocratic medicine to the interpretation of history; and to the demonstration of this the rest of this chapter must be devoted.

The commentators have noted that Thucydides was keenly interested in natural phenomena, and have collected examples of his observations, e.g. of eclipses, tidal waves, the whirlpool of Charybdis, the silting up of the Acheloüs mouth, volcanic action at Stromboli and Aetna, forest fires, and the effects of the plague on flora and fauna at Athens. They have further observed that in each and every case he sought a natural explanation of the phenomenon in question. But Herodotus had already, in his disquisition on the topography of the Thessalian plain, provided a model for the rational explanation of natural phenomena, when he remarked (vii. 129) that the gap at the mouth of the Peneius river is the work of an earthquake and consequently that those who like to call earthquakes the work of Poseidon may do so. Thucydides, therefore, cannot be credited with originality in this field; although one may

[1] *Œuvres d'Hippocrate*, i. 474.

notice in passing that his grip on the principle of the uniformity of nature is firmer than that of his predecessor. Herodotus, in default of a plausible natural explanation, may sometimes be tempted to take refuge in supernaturalism. Thucydides never yields to superstition. Ignorant, for example, though he be of the real causes of the solar eclipse, he is content to state the observable facts, that this phenomenon occurs only at the beginning of the lunar month; confident that the eclipse has no supernatural significance, and that in due course will be made the generalization which will explain the phenomenon to the satisfaction of scientific minds (ii. 28).

The originality of Thucydides lies rather in his attempt to bring *all human action* within the realm of natural causes. In this connexion should be noticed the peculiar word πρόφασις which he uses to designate a 'natural cause'. This word, which in Homer, Herodotus, and later writers unquestionably connotes 'formulated reason' or 'pretext', means in Thucydides 'exciting cause' or the 'physical antecedent of a physical state'. To Cornford πρόφασις has proved a stumbling-block; it is one of the foundation stones upon which he builds his theory of Thucydides *Myth*-historicus. Other commentators, impressed with its apparently obvious meaning in Thucydides, have argued that, in this as in other cases, etymology must give way to common sense. The fact is that the word, as used by the historian, is in the highest degree technical. It is uniformly used by Hippocrates in the sense of 'exciting cause', and has been taken over directly by Thucydides in his attempt to apply the methods of medicine to history; the adaptation of methods involving, as is usual, the adoption of terminology.[1]

In Thucydides, then, as in Hippocrates, it is assumed that all human actions and sufferings are subject to natural causes,

[1] The Rev. E. M. Walker, of Queen's College, Oxford, in his lectures, 1911–13, pointed out that πρόφασις in the medical writers was the regular word for cause; but whether he ever went beyond the dictionary meaning of the word, I cannot say. A somewhat parallel adoption of medical terminology is the use of κατάστασις. Hippocrates, *Epidemics*, employs the word to designate the general conditions prevailing at the outbreak of an epidemic. The political writers adopt it in the modern sense of the word 'state'. Plat. *Rep.* 426 c ἡ κατάστασις τῆς πόλεως. 547 B ἡ κατάστασις τῆς δημοκρατίας. Isoc. 38 B ἡ παροῦσα κατάστασις.

and by these are meant the causes that are proper to human nature. In other words, both writers accept *men* no less than *things* as ultimates for the purposes of historical as of medical science. To Cornford this appears as a grave defect. He says :[1] 'If we would understand Thucydides we must not regard a human action as partly caused by innumerable influences of environment, and by events that happened before the agent was born, right back into an immeasurable past. . . . The world upon which the Greek looked presented no such spectacle as this. Human affairs—the subject-matter of history—were not to him a single strand in the illimitable web of natural evolution; their course was shaped solely by one or both of two factors : immediate human motives and the will of gods and spirits, of Fortune, or of Fate. The rationalist who rejected the second class was left with the first alone—the original and uncaused acts of human wills.' The modern passion for reducing history to mechanics could hardly go farther than this. But surely Hippocrates and Thucydides are entitled, for the purposes of their science, to lay down their own postulates; and to admit if they so desire, specifically 'psychical' alongside of 'material' causes as ultimate factors for history. Again Cornford[2] appears to go too far when he remarks that the ancients 'looked simply and solely to the feelings, motives, characters of individuals or of cities. These and (apart from supernatural agencies) these only, appeared to them to shape the course of human history.' The observations, quoted above from *Airs, Waters, Places* effectually dispose of such a view. To Hippocrates the ultimate factors were human motives in relation to environment, institutional as well as geographical. In his study of the evolution of Greek society at the beginning of the first book, Thucydides takes the cue and applies the Hippocratean principle to the elucidation of past as well as present, with such brilliance that the passage may truly be described as one of the greatest, as it is one of the earliest studies in human geography to be found in European literature.[3]

To embark on a detailed examination of Thucydides' psychology would take us too far afield. It is sufficient to say

[1] Op. cit., p. 67.   [2] p. 66.   [3] See chapter iv below, p. 37 ff.

that, like Hippocrates, Thucydides regards human nature as a relatively uniform and stable entity, in which, for purposes of analysis, one may distinguish γνώμη, the intelligence which affords direction to the activities of the organism, and the various potentialities (δυνάμεις) which unfold in response to their respective stimuli, and result in various changes (μεταβολαί) which make for the well-being of the organism or otherwise.[1] Here may be noted how modern is the psychology of Thucydides in contrast with the classical or 'faculty' psychology which was derived from Platonism, in that he stresses the unity of the organism in the response which it makes to any particular stimulus (iii. 45. 7). 'In a word then, it is impossible and absurd to suppose that, when human nature is subjected to a powerful urge in any direction, it can be diverted either by force of law, or by any other terror.' Again (iii. 45. 1), 'Yet carried away by hope, they take the risk of [rebelling against Athens]. No one ever condemns himself to death in advance, when he embarks on a dangerous enterprise'. This last passage illustrates how, according to Thucydidean psychology, judgement tends to reinforce desire, so that the resultant act is an act of the whole personality.

Thus personality counts as a factor in human history, and has to be taken into account in the explanation of events. Spontaneous combustion may account for forest fires (ii. 77. 4), but to explain the downfall of the Athenian Empire are needed the personalities of Cleon, Nicias, and Alcibiades, each of whom, in his own way, made his unwitting contribution to that catastrophe. Thucydides therefore parades them across the stage, not in order to abuse them or praise them, still less to gratify the idle curiosity of the casual reader with a mirror of statesmen, but simply in order that he may bring out the facts and ideas connected with them which are relevant to the analysis upon which his eye is steadily fixed.

On the other hand, the growth of society is no more spontaneous than its destruction. As Hippocrates had said, growth is the result of shock which stimulates the mind and awakens it from stagnation. Such shocks, Thucydides observes, as

[1] See especially iii. 82.

though developing the Hippocratean thesis, are those that come from the struggle for control of the valleys, resulting in the successive organizations of power which culminate in the *polis*, or the clash of cultures resulting from invasion, or the fusion of immigrant with native as in the case of Thesean Athens. No less significant are the accumulations of capital, which suggest to their possessors all sorts of possibilities hitherto undreamed of; and the invention of ships and the art of navigation, which constitute the foundations of historical Greece. In all cases, where new ideas are involved, it is assumed that these ideas were born in somebody's brain. Thus Ameinocles of Corinth appears as the man who invented the trireme and later introduced it into Samos. Similarly with the idea of consolidation (συνοικισμός). In Athens this did not come about spontaneously, but was the work of Theseus, a man of power as well as wisdom.[1] Theseus, stimulated by the existence of perils which arose not merely from foreign incursions but also from mutual quarrels among the village communities in Attica, and working by means of persuasion mingled with force, imposed on the inhabitants of the peninsula a unitary organization which afterwards got the sanction of religion; and deserved it, because indeed it saved the Athenians not only from foreigners but also from themselves. One is reminded of the observation of Hippocrates, quoted above, that there is an element of compulsion connected with *nomos*, but that *nature* ultimately comes in to reinforce it, so that it becomes indeed a sort of second nature itself. And one may suppose that consolidation, which was in Athens brought about as the response to certain conditions, came about in Argos and elsewhere, if not in response to the same conditions, at least to conditions equally compelling, or was introduced according to the self-same law of imitation which led the Samians to copy the naval architecture of the people of Corinth, and which to this day prompts progressive individuals and nations to import and adopt the advanced ideas of their rivals.

The power of innovation or 'invention' is one of the subjects which most engage the attention of Thucydides, and one

[1] ii. 15. 2 Θησεύς, γενόμενος μετὰ τοῦ ξυνετοῦ καὶ δυνατός.

which he discusses in various passages. In their speech at
Sparta (i. 68–71), the Corinthians charge the Spartans with
apathy and stagnation, and apparently attribute these defects
of character to the peculiarity of the environment of Lycurgan
institutions.[1] On the other hand (70. 2) the Athenians are
represented as innovators, quick to conceive an idea and to
execute the plans which they conceive, beyond their powers
daring, prepared to gamble beyond their judgement, in the
moment of peril sustained by hope, venturing fearlessly abroad,
etc.; so that (§ 9) in short, if one said that they were born
neither to take any rest themselves or to allow it to other men,
one would speak the mere truth. These characteristics, which
constituted such a menace to the conservative states of Greece,
are (71. 2) referred to the atmosphere and institutions of Athens.
'Your institutions,' the Corinthians say, 'compared with those
of the Athenians, are out of date.'

The nature and purpose of the speeches in Thucydides must
be reserved for later treatment. Meanwhile, it may be noted
that Thucydides either shared with Pericles or was prepared to
attribute to him a point of view substantially the same as that
which he puts into the mouth of the Corinthians in the passage
just quoted. In the *Funeral Speech* Pericles accounts for the
unique qualities of his fellow citizens in precisely the same way,
viz. as a result of the spiritual atmosphere created in Athens
by the great generation to which Themistocles belonged, and
maintained in ever increasing power and volume by their
successors. The specific points which he makes, reminding one
again of *Airs, Waters, Places*, are worth noting:

(1) The Athenians are autochthonous, and the natural product of the peculiar geographical conditions in the Attic
peninsula.[2]

(2) The shock of the Persian War gave Athens the first
great impulse towards her imperial destiny. While Sparta and
other conservative Greek states failed to rise to the occasion,
and to effect those adaptations necessary to meet the new

---

[1] i. 68. 1 τὸ πιστὸν τῆς καθ' ὑμᾶς αὐτοὺς πολιτείας καὶ ὁμιλίας.

[2] Cf. i. 2. 6 and ii. 14–17, where the social evolution of the country-
side is more fully described.

conditions created by the war, the empire-builders of Athens seized their opportunity and created the empire, which not without toil and stress they handed on to the succeeding generation.[1]

(3) The empire, as they possessed it, was the consequence of the atmosphere, social and political, of Athens.[2]

With regard to the question of innovation—the capacity for conceiving and applying new ideas in human life—Thucydides in two passages, speaking in his own person, reveals his opinion. The first passage is in the estimate of Themistocles (i. 138. 3–6), the second, in the estimate of Pericles (ii. 65); and, of these, the former is the more significant. In the *Funeral Speech* also (ii. 37) it is argued that the spirit of equality in Athens is not inimical to distinction, that, in fact, so far from implying a cult of mediocrity, it actually makes provision for the employment of talent (ἀρετή) wherever it may be found. The existence of talent—special endowment—Thucydides was prepared to recognize; whether it was the peculiar abilities of an Antiphon, or an Alcibiades, or even a Cleon,[3] or the more normal qualities of a Demosthenes or a Brasidas, each of whom played his part in weaving the web of history, so that account has to be taken of him by the judicious historian. Accordingly, in the contribution of formative ideas to the life of the community, some men, such as Pericles and Themistocles, stood pre-eminently above their fellows. The latter, in whose fertile brain the idea of empire was first conceived, seems to have fascinated Thucydides. In estimating his contribution to Athenian life, he protested against the somewhat unfavourable verdict of Herodotus. Employing the current formulae of sophistic analysis, nature and nurture (φύσις and τέχνη or, as he says, μελέτη), he reveals his belief that while nurture may save men from mediocrity, it can never account for genius. For the significance of Themistocles lay precisely in the revelation

---

[1] ii. 36. 2 κτησάμενοι γὰρ πρὸς οἷς ἐδέξαντο ὅσην ἔχομεν ἀρχὴν οὐκ ἀπόνως ἡμῖν τοῖς νῦν προσκατέλιπον.

[2] § 4 ἀπὸ δὲ οἴας τε ἐπιτηδεύσεως ἤλθομεν ἐπ᾽ αὐτὰ καὶ μεθ᾽ οἴας πολιτείας καὶ τρόπων ἐξ οἴων μεγάλα ἐγένετο.

[3] iii. 36. 6 βιαιότατος τῶν πολιτῶν τῷ τε δήμῳ παρὰ πολὺ ἐν τῷ τότε πιθανώτατος.

which he gave of the strength of natural genius.[1] Without the advantages of a protracted education, but by the sheer force of his genius, he was in fact supreme in his ability to extemporize expedients to meet the necessities of the day.[2] This is the answer which Thucydides makes to those (like Cornford) who complain that he makes too much of the 'uncaused actions of human will'. For history, talent—especially insight and penetration ($\gamma\nu\omega\mu\eta$)—is, like human nature itself, original and ultimately inexplicable, a postulate in fact necessary to the science. Thus did Thucydides dispose of the question of mind in evolution; and his authority survived to create the psychological interpretation of history common to the greatest of subsequent classical historians. For us in our day it has remained to essay the task of dehumanizing the history of humanity.

Thucydides was a child of Periclean Athens, and the intense individualism of the age in which he lived made it natural for him, perhaps, to consider the problem of society and of history from the point of view of the relationship of individuals to the group. Accordingly, Thucydides is never tempted to conceive of society itself as an organism—and so far his point of view would meet with acceptance by 'realistic' sociologists of the present day. On the other hand, he was evidently impressed with the attempt in Periclean Athens to unify the interests and sentiments of the individual and the group, and he was no less impressed with the fatal failure to do so in the case, not merely of Alcibiades, but of the less spectacular conservative and ultra-reactionary landed classes with which he himself was connected. In one respect his individualistic prepossessions seem to have exposed him to the just criticism of the commentators, that is, in his account of the evolution of society in primitive Greece. The canons of interpretation which he employs in this field are exactly the same as he employs in his analysis of current history; and so he seems to have accepted the historicity of legendary figures like Agamemnon

---

[1] i. 138. 3 βεβαιότατα δὴ φύσεως ἰσχὺν δηλώσας καὶ διαφερόντως τι ἐς αὐτὸ μᾶλλον ἑτέρου ἄξιος θαυμάσαι.

[2] Ib. φύσεως μὲν δυνάμει, μελέτης δὲ βραχύτητι κράτιστος δὴ οὗτος αὐτοσχεδιάζειν τὰ δέοντα ἐγένετο.

and Minos, the latter of whom, say How and Wells,[1] he makes into a prehistoric Pericles. We may note in passing that he guards himself from dogmatism by referring constantly to the merely traditional character of his authorities.[2] Nevertheless, in his reconstruction of early Greek history it is probable that Thucydides allowed himself to be carried away to some extent by the experience of his own day. A fifth-century Athenian could hardly have imagined a society like that of medieval Europe. He failed equally to appreciate the strength of the religious motive in the still undifferentiated society of primitive Greece. However, this at least is clear, that, in his treatment of prehistoric Greece, Thucydides fell victim to the formulation of an induction on too narrow a foundation of fact; for the individualism of the fifth century B.C. cannot be regarded as in any degree universal, though perhaps it is normal in developed societies. But it was not his method, so much as the inadequacy of the facts at his disposal, which was at fault.

The reconstruction of a past, remote whether in time or, more significantly, in spirit, may seem at best a hopeless task; and, as the real triumph of Thucydides lay in contemporary history, we gladly turn to his work in that field. The view of human motivation, which he appears to have held in common with Hippocrates, has already been examined. Beyond this, all belongs for the historian to the realm of τύχη or chance. Philosophy may, but science cannot know of any 'cause' capable of bringing to pass the plague in Athens at a critical moment in her history, or of any 'cause' capable of producing that fatal eclipse of the moon which completely immobilized the already terrified men of Athens at the last moment when escape was still possible from the hands of a vengeful and relentless foe. For history these are and must remain mere coincidences. Therefore, to those who accept the self-denying ordinance of history they must be relegated to the realm of τύχη—the incalculable. It is important to notice that in these, as in other cases, it is the coincidence itself which does not yield to any form of prognostication. Hippocrates (*Airs*, ii) had already remarked that the contribution of astronomy to medicine was

[1] *Herodotus*, i., p. 32.　　[2] i. 4. 1 ἀκοῇ ἴσμεν.

anything but insignificant, on account of the effect which celestial events have on the *diseases* and the *digestive organs* of mankind. Similarly, the effect of the plague at Athens upon the morale of the Athenians is a proper subject of scientific investigation; and at the same time the plague itself is traced to a natural cause, in contagion, through the Piraeus from Egypt. The coincidence of events, however, remains inexplicable. Accordingly, while theologians and philosophers may dispute regarding the ultimate meaning of such coincidence, as Polybius does about the coincidences that in his day laid the Mediterranean world at the feet of Rome, or Sallust (in his letter to Caesar *de Ordinanda Republica*) about the coincidences that in their turn brought the Roman world beneath the heel of the dictator, the truly scientific historian, limited by his self-imposed method, can do nothing but hold his peace.

Scientific history, as Thucydides argues (i. 20–2), has nothing in common with imaginative literature, but consists in the diligent and unremitting search for truth, and it has its own standards of evidence (τεκμήρια καὶ σημεῖα) similar to the evidences of medicine, which are under favourable conditions adequate (ἀποχρώντως). The truths of history like those of medicine consist first in the actual transactions which have taken place (τὰ ἔργα τῶν πραχθέντων); and these, even if they are subjects of first-hand knowledge, should be accepted only after most careful check with the results of independent observations. Next come the λόγοι, or formulations—summaries and at the same time interpretations—in so far as these entered into and affected the course of events. With regard to the transactions themselves, Thucydides notes in true scientific fashion the common dangers to which the historian is exposed, the psychological perils arising from moral bias, defective recollection, as well as the carelessness and lack of observation characteristic of mankind. In the case of the λόγοι the difficulties of the historian are more acute.

For in the λόγοι, the permanently valuable elements of his work, Thucydides faced the problem, not merely of reporting correctly what was actually said on each occasion, but of amplifying and developing these statements in a manner

appropriate to the occasion. To the modern historian, this may
seem a strange kind of realism; actually in the hands of Thucydides this quaint literary convention, which Herodotus had
carried over from the epic or the drama, affords an admirable
vehicle for the expression of those points of view, always partial,
frequently conflicting, which determined the transactions—
the great issues, in short, of the war and the mainsprings of
human action in relation thereto. The *Funeral Speech* then, and
all the other speeches, represent the thought of Thucydides just
as they are expressed in language which is unquestionably his
own. But in another sense they are genuinely objective, in so
far as each of them constitutes an analysis conveying to the
reader the attitude of representative individuals or groups
in relation to the facts which came up for discussion. To state
the facts and formulate the issues, this appears to have been the
aim of Thucydides. Thus he was almost always enabled to
avoid dogmatic judgements in his own person. And if the facts
are well authenticated and the points of view are fairly and
adequately represented, the device enables the historian to
withdraw from the picture, leaving the reader to judge for
himself. If this was Thucydides' aim, he appears amply to
have achieved it, as witness the controversies which in modern
times the commentators have waged regarding the significance
of the war.

The λόγοι, therefore, represent the attempt of Thucydides to
do for history what Hippocrates was at the same time trying to
do for medicine—the attempt, that is, to establish such classi-
fications or formulations (τὰ εἴδη) as would raise history from
the level of mere chronicle, characteristic of the annalists
(λογογράφοι), just as in medicine the same formulations were
needed if medical science was to escape from the mere empiricism of the Cnidian school. Through the symptoms to
arrive at a general description and thence to penetrate, if
possible, to the true classification of the malady, this is the procedure which Hippocrates advocates and which he designates
by the words *semeiology* and *prognosis*. But this was the very
process which Thucydides sought to apply to history, which thus
for him becomes the semeiology and prognosis of human life.

The unforgettable picture of the plague at Athens, copied by Lucretius and imitated by Procopius in ancient, as it was by Gibbon in modern times, has always been accepted as one of the best illustrations of Thucydides' temperament, the keenness with which he observed concrete fact, the cold detachment with which he reported the symptoms of a malady to which he himself had fallen victim, the precise analytical power with which he portrayed the changes (μεταβολαί), not merely bodily but also mental, of the disease. For the commentators generally the account of the plague has illustrated these characteristics. For us it does more; it constitutes the most intimate link between Thucydides and Hippocrates, and seems indeed to be the bridge between the two.

In his account of the plague Thucydides follows precisely the Hippocratic procedure. After the general introduction (ii. 47–8), in which he describes the outbreak and its gravity, he begins (49) by what in Hippocratic terminology is a κατάστασις—a general description of the conditions, climatic and otherwise, prevailing during the summer in which the plague broke out. Then follows the general description of symptoms, including a reference (§ 6) to the fact that the 'crisis' occurred as a rule on the seventh or ninth day. Now there is no feature of Hippocratic theory more striking than this notion that every malady tends to run a normal course up to a crisis, which once surmounted, the patient normally recovers. So Thucydides, having dealt with the course of the disease up to its crisis, goes on (§§ 6–7) to describe what may be called the complications attending recovery. Such, he concludes, is the general description or semeiology of the epidemic.[1] With regard to its classification or prognosis, unfortunately no rational account can be given.[2] For, contrary to normal experience, the affliction spread to beast and bird, and also (51. 2) there was no specific remedy, so to speak, the application of which assured relief. Then, too, it smote all alike (51. 3) whatever had been their medical history or their regimen of life.[3] Thus this epidemic

---

[1] ii. 51. 1 τὸ μὲν νόσημα . . . τοιοῦτον ἦν ἐπὶ πᾶν τὴν ἰδέαν . . .
[2] ii. 50. 1 γενόμενον γὰρ κρεῖσσον λόγου τὸ εἶδος τῆς νόσου.
[3] Cf. *Ancient Medicine*, iii, on δίαιτη.

eluded rational classification from every point of view. The passage incidentally throws light on the Thucydidean conception of πρόγνωσις: what is 'classification' and how is it possible?

Hippocratean prognosis, after the general description of symptoms, usually includes an account of psychical reactions. In his attempt, indeed, to relate psychical manifestations to the physical constitution, Hippocrates is generally credited with having developed the theory of the four primary humours, of health as a blending of these in due proportions relative to the organism, and of disease as a disturbance, normally resulting from a failure in the process of assimilation (πέψις). Accordingly, Thucydides proceeds to record the depression and hopelessness that settle down on the patient, when the presence of the disease is detected, as well as his vain elation when the crisis is successfully passed, and the hope, scientifically groundless,[1] that he would never perish of any other disease. He notices also the effect of the situation upon those who, themselves not having as yet fallen victims, either feared to approach the sufferers, or if they did so, paid the penalty of their unselfish idealism (51. 5) with their lives.

In the Hippocratean sense, the plague was an unparalleled shock, and *likely* therefore to be the occasion of derangements (μεταβολαί) equally unparalleled. Such was indeed the case, and (53) Thucydides goes on to describe the general outbreak of social anarchy and demoralization which was its result—an outbreak in which the most evil passions of human nature were released, and which human law proved as powerless as divine authority to check. Thus neither Hellenic religion nor Periclean statesmanship sufficed to provide safeguards adequate to meet the shock (§ 4).

The canons of interpretation employed for the prognosis of the plague seem to us to be the canons employed also in the interpretation of Greek history generally. For Thucydides, the evolution of society is determined by a principle which, in contradistinction, on the one hand to materialism, and on the other to idealism, we venture to designate as that of

[1] ii. 51. 6 ἐλπίς . . . κούφη. Does any vague notion of 'immunity' underlie this 'groundless hope' in the popular mind?

'physical determinism'.[1] Logically, perhaps, following the classification of Aristotle, causes may be distinguished as 'material', 'formal', 'efficient', and 'final'; but it should be remembered that these distinctions had not yet been made when Thucydides wrote; and it may be questioned whether, from the point of view of historical interpretation, they were or are of any great value. For, from the standpoint of science, the kind of 'formal' and 'final' causes which have been employed have proved useless; because such causes are not susceptible of observation and verification by scientific procedure. But, in any case, science does not raise itself by its own bootstraps; and there is no possible demonstration, scientifically speaking, of the existence either of nature or of God. *Natural causes* there are, unless man is a madman living in a madhouse; and these are at one and the same time 'material' and 'efficient'. For example, when Thucydides attributes the beginnings of the city state to the accumulation of capital, he does not mean to imply that the 'material', whether it be land, cattle, slaves, or hard cash, is what determines the course of evolution. These things, to him, constitute capital in so far as their meaning and significance are appreciated by their possessors. In other words, he is thinking in terms analogous to those employed in the parable of the Talents. The man without a sense of the value of his possession buries it in the earth. His fellow, conscious of what may be done with his, puts it to work and makes it bear fruit. The just sense of value, which enables the prudent speculator to size up the situation and to manipulate with profit the forces at his disposal, is the same sense of value which Thucydides attributes to personalities like Themistocles and Pericles. Carlyle, exaggerating no doubt the significance of great personalities, turns history itself into the biographies of its great men. Thucydides is perhaps more judicious, and never forgets to relate genius to the circumstances which give it an opportunity for free play. Thus in another age Nicias, with his conventional morality, might have exercised a salutary influence

---

[1] 'Physical', following the usage of Hippocrates and Thucydides. Modern usage perversely seeks to restrict the meaning of this word to that of 'the world with man left out'.

on the fortunes of his country. As a politician, however, in democratic and imperialist Athens, and as the reluctant leader of her forces in an enterprise which he loathed, his very virtues proved pernicious and contributed to the disaster which he had sought so studiously to avoid. This is not to say that in politics there is no morality; yet it does imply that political situations may arise in which a man can be *too moral*, or rather that in certain situations the rules of conventional morality can with difficulty be applied. In such situations, the advice of Plato is, characteristically, that the 'good' man should take refuge under the wall. In this connexion, the function of the scientist is to state the observable facts; while once more theologian and philosopher may speculate regarding the mysterious ways of Providence or Fate.

Thus, while Fate or Providence rewards each man according to his desert, the only 'moral' which the historian can draw is that it is necessary to cultivate that mysterious power of insight, which science postulates as a natural endowment of individuals and peoples. Thus the problem of the social physician becomes a problem of finding appropriate nourishment (δίαιτα or τροφή), we shall not say for the soul, but for the constitution (φύσις) of man; and we shall see in the following chapter how the problem of doing so is faced, as Thucydides sees it, by Sparta and Athens, and in each case with what observable results.

For it is noteworthy that in both cases the problem is faced, and that both the system of liberty and the system of authority are represented as positive prescriptions of a definite and intelligible regimen of life. Athenian liberalism, no less than Spartan authoritarianism, is far removed in spirit and in practice from the optimistic liberalism or anarchism of modern times. Neither Hippocrates nor, presumably, Thucydides ever supposed that 'nature', if left to herself, could work the miracle of cure.

He, however, who looks for a positive statement of Thucydides' own views on this subject, will look in vain; for the pages of Thucydides contain no ready-made system of social therapeutics. Hippocrates had divided the work of the physician into three parts: semeiology, prognosis, and therapeutics. Semeiology and prognosis are really two aspects of the same process. They include at one and the same time the accurate observation and the intelligent appreciation of data. Thus the mechanical notion of 'induction', by which one is supposed first to collect the data and then to generalize from them, is not Hippocratic, and whoever of the moderns may desire to have the credit of discovering 'induction' may do so. To Hippocrates, as to Thucydides, it is obvious that if you set about collecting pebbles in order to make a generalization from them, you must have in your mind the rough idea of a pebble to start with, otherwise it may turn out that after all you have been collecting eggs or apples instead of pebbles. Thus the function of semeiology and prognosis is simply to widen the connotation of the class (τὸ εἶδος) or, in other words, it is not a mechanical and passive, but an active mental process, and this is what makes it a capacity which few in the highest degree enjoy, so that, exemplified in a Themistocles, it is a subject for admiration. Thus scientific history makes no attempt to rob life of its great mystery. It accepts the fact of natural endowment as an essential condition of well-being and progress; at the same time noting the comparative rarity of its occurrence in any very full measure; and the consequence for mankind of those great inventions which spring from the brains of its possessors.

The scientific historian, as such, limits himself to the semeiology and prognosis of society; leaving to the political philosopher the task of constructing, on the basis of this prognosis, an adequate system of social therapeutics. This, then, is the real reason for many of the peculiarities of Thucydides which the commentators have noted and for which they have tried to account. His 'objectivity' and 'detachment' are results of the scientific method which he consciously adopts, and seeks conscientiously to apply. This, rather than the circumstances of his birth and life—his mixed descent, his affiliation with the conservatives, his exile by the democrats—enables him to characterize his native country, and put his finger with unerring precision on both the strength and weakness of imperial democracy. Moreover, his reticence is the reticence of relevancy.

His duty is to consider the significance of personalities and events, in strict relation to his purpose. Hence those silences in regard to what happened, if the events had no bearing on the particular issue under discussion, which after all distinguish history from annals. Hence also those partial portraits or sketches of personalities, so vivid as far as they go, but yet so irritating to the modern, with his habit of discursive reading and of discursive writing. These, also, are in strict keeping with scientific method, and serve to distinguish history from biography. Finally, it is vain to look in the pages of Thucydides for any systematic statement of his beliefs. The good social physician will, in prognosis, keep strictly to the task of writing the 'history' of his patients, and he will reserve his schemes of social therapeutics for special treatment later, if he himself essays the task of treatment.

Yet, to all who accept the method of science, i.e. the view that life itself is the real teacher of mankind, so that it is necessary to consider how men do as a fact behave, before considering how they should, the one task is the necessary preliminary of the other. Such a conviction may without doubt be attributed to Thucydides; therein lies for him and for those who think with him the usefulness of history.

If this point of view be accepted, it limits decisively the scope and nature of social science. Sociologists, as such, should cease to look in history for anything except observable physical causes; and they should no longer attempt to extract from the study of society any *general* law of progress, as they have long since ceased to find in history any general law of decline, and as, in modern times, few or none of them profess to discover in it evidence for a law of cycles. To do otherwise is to violate the first principle of scientific method, as laid down by the author of *Ancient Medicine*, and applied by Thucydides to sociology—to confuse the 'is' with the 'ought'—in short, to disguise what is really philosophy in the gown of science. For it was against the general hypothesis that the author of *Ancient Medicine* had levelled the full weight of his artillery, seeking to demolish this citadel as the necessary preliminary to genuine science. It is both the right and the duty of science to speak in terms of limited and concrete ends. History, for instance, may properly consider the 'progress' of Rome under the principate in the direction of centralized and bureaucratic autocracy; or it may consider the decline of the city state from a condition of independence and self-sufficiency to that of a mere municipality under the imperialism of Alexander or of Rome. But to the questions: 'what constitutes progress or decline in general, how do these come about, and how may they be measured?' history returns no answer. These are general hypotheses, utterly unverifiable by observation; that is, they belong to the realm of philosophy, and not to the field of history and social science.

The word 'history' is full of ambiguity, and this is not surprising, because of the various senses in which the word is commonly used. We shall not speak of those to whom the record of the past is quite without meaning, although there is perhaps an increasing number of such. Apart from them, there are many people who regard history as a record once and for all delivered to the saints. For them, this record is sacred, and no considerations of truth are allowed to disturb the source from which they draw nourishment to feed their favourite prejudices. To others, history is merely material for propaganda. Unconscious, perhaps, of the sharp distinction between 'historical' and 'imaginative' literature, or, it may be, despairing of the possibility of an accurate interpretation of the past, they do not hesitate to 'reconstruct' history by the suppression of features which are unpleasant or disagreeable to them; and thus Clio is prostituted to the cause of world-peace, or progress, or whatever worthy or unworthy cause they desire to foster. There are, however, still others who follow Thucydides in regarding history as the diligent and unremitting search for truth, and who combine the most profound respect for the 'facts', in so far as these can be discovered, with the attempt to interpret these facts, as the physician endeavours to interpret the symptoms of his patient. To these history is really the equivalent of political science. In the present chapter we have endeavoured to set forth the method of this science as Thucydides saw it. In subsequent chapters we shall attempt to illustrate the fruits of the method, as he uses it for (*a*) the prognosis of power (social welfare as realized in state and empire), and (*b*) the prognosis of weakness, or the pathology of society. Besides illustrating certain results which the scientific method yields, this survey will perhaps serve to demonstrate its limitations, especially in relation to what may be described as the philosophical method of approaching the same profound questions.

IV
THE STATE

PLATO, and those who follow him in employing the method of philosophy as opposed to that of science, visualize society from the point of view of *general* well-being, and thus for them the social question becomes: what are the essentials necessary to constitute a spiritual home for the ideal man? Aristotle, in the famous sentence (*Pol.* 1252^b 30) in which he says that 'the state comes into existence to satisfy the bare needs of life, and continues for the sake of the good life', begins as a scientist, but ends as a philosopher. For, as has already been remarked, science takes life itself for granted. Its object is to observe and classify the various means by which life is propagated and maintained, and on the other hand destroyed or transmuted into other forms. But to pass from *specific* to *general* ends is, for the scientist, illegitimate. The moment he does so he leaves the solid ground of observable fact, and trespasses on the territory of religion and philosophy. For, if it be asked in connexion with the 'good' life: good for what? the answer can only be: 'good' for the Aristotelian man. Thus the touchstones turn out to be moral and spiritual, and we find ourselves at once in the realm of universal ends and values, which is utterly beyond the world of science. On the other hand, *scientific* ethics, like *scientific* history, must inevitably be utilitarian, in the sense that it limits itself to the observation of those facts which are demonstrably 'useful' to the individual and to the race; and herein, it may be thought, lies the great weakness of all systems of ethics and politics constructed from scientific data; for they have not, in spite of their efforts, succeeded in accounting for the ideas of truth, beauty, and holiness; and because of the self-imposed limitations of scientific method, by which science confines itself to the examination of specific ends and values, they are never likely to do so.

In view of these considerations, it is not surprising that Thucydides as a scientific inquirer connects the beginnings of

society with the methods adopted for the acquisition of food
and shelter, these being specific means for ensuring the pro-
pagation and maintenance of life; and that, in his examination
of the evolution of Greek society in its distinctive forms, he
consistently avoids general teleology, and limits himself to the
consideration of observable phenomena, in relation to their
'physical' causes. One does not have to be a modern food-
chemist to appreciate, roughly at any rate, the specific value
of food to the organism; and the earliest of the Hippocratics
had already outlined the evolution of a practical science of diet.
'I hold', he says,[1] 'that not even the mode of living and nourishment practised at the present time by healthy individuals would
have been discovered, had a man been satisfied with eating and
drinking the same things as satisfy an ox, a horse, and all
organisms except mankind, for example, the products of the
earth—fruits, wood, and grass. On these they are nourished,
grow and live without pain, and they require no additional diet
of any kind. To begin with, in my opinion, mankind also
utilized the same kind of food; and our present ways of living
have been discovered and developed over a long period of time.
. . . In primitive times, people probably suffered less [from the
crudity of such diet] because they were accustomed to it, but
even then they suffered severely. *The majority, possessing a weak
constitution, probably perished, while the strong resisted longer,*
just as in modern times some men easily assimilate strong foods,
while others do so only with many severe pains. Accordingly,
for this reason, primitive man, I think, sought for nourishment
that harmonized with his constitution and discovered the forms
of diet which we enjoy at the present day. Thus from wheat,
after steeping, winnowing, grinding, sifting, kneading, and
baking it, men produced bread, and from barley they produced
cake. By way of experiment (πρηγματευσάμενοι), they boiled and
baked and mixed many other things, and they combined the
strong, unmixed ingredients with the weaker, adapting them
in all cases to the constitution and capacity of mankind, because
they considered that, in the case of those elements which are too
powerful for the constitution to assimilate if taken into the

[1] *Ancient Medicine*, ch. iii.

system, from these come pain, disease, and death, but from such as it can assimilate follow nourishment, growth, and health.'

Thus, in the opinion of the author, a process of natural selection determined for primitive man the essentials of a diet adapted to his constitution, while, at the same time, the nascent intelligence of mankind was, by the use of rough empirical methods, establishing one of the first and most elementary contacts between himself and his environment. That this penetrating generalization of the author is correct is confirmed by evidence which accumulates from studying the debris of primitive religion, not merely in connexion with the cults of early fertility gods but, more significantly, in the attribution to deities like Athene of inventions such as the cultivation of the olive, and the first notions of scientific agriculture.

All this, and more, is implied, if not actually stated, in those remarkable chapters (i. 1–19) in which Thucydides sketches the evolution of Greek society in its characteristic and peculiar forms. Such omissions as occur in this powerful reconstruction of the past are probably due, apart from the extraordinary compression of the narrative, to the fact that the author aims to depict the rise not of civilization as a whole,[1] but rather of the distinctive features of Hellenic polity. 'One could point', he says (i. 6. 6), 'to many other characteristics in which the life of primitive Greece resembles that of the present-day barbarism.' Thucydides' starting-point is therefore tribal or family and clan society, and his first problem is to show how this, in the peculiar environment of the Hellenic world, evolved into political society, properly so called, i.e. the society of the city state.

Naturally enough, he connects this phase of social evolution with certain innovations adopted for the accumulation and preservation of the food supply. For the selection of food, as the Hippocratic treatise implies, involves the acquisition and protection of stocks suitable in quality and in quantity for all possible contingencies. But stocks of this character, especially

---

[1] Lucretius (v. 783 ff.) sketches the rise of civilization generally, according to the spirit and method of atomistic philosophy.

of cereals and fruits, require cultivation; and cultivation was
difficult, if not impossible, amid the various and immense
hazards to which life in primitive times was exposed. Thus,
even in early Greece (i. 2), men lived a life but little removed
from that of nomads, without fixed habitation and subject
continuously to the pressure of larger groups. They neither
possessed accumulated stocks nor did they plant the land with
fruit trees (φυτεύω), and, as their agricultural efforts did not
go beyond a mere scratching of the soil, they lived a mere hand-
to-mouth existence. In these conditions, the naturally fruitful
valleys, which in Greece of course are limited in number and
extent, became the object of general desire; and stronger groups,
envying the weaker their possession of these valleys, successively
invaded and occupied them, until they themselves in turn were
ejected.

Conditions, however, were altered when groups here and
there, who had accumulated a small surplus, resolved to stand
fast and unite to protect their own; for this was the beginning
of a general transition from the unwalled and defenceless village
community based on kin, to the 'state' properly so called, with
a unitary organization and a citizenship in which the bond of
territorial contiguity and common interest replaced the tie of
birth. If, however, one may generalize from the case of Athens
(ii. 14–15), 'consolidation' did not occur immediately as an
alternative to the autonomous kin-association of the village,
but there was an intermediate stage in which groups of villages
federated for the purely occasional purposes of defence.
Nevertheless it remains true that, according to Thucydides, the
beginnings of the state coincided with the beginnings of capital,
and that both were responses to definite and critical human
needs. And the περιουσία χρημάτων is truly capital, because,
though as yet it includes no medium of exchange, it represents
the fruit of the first deliberate attempts to develop (φυτεύω)
and exploit (νέμω) the earth, and is the surplus resulting from
such exploitation. Scientifically speaking, therefore, the 'state'
is natural as 'capital' is natural, because each corresponds to
fundamental needs inherent in the constitution of man, though
in neither case is the 'natural' the merely spontaneous and

primitive. Man, as man, has always been a *thinker*, and what links the splendid structure of developed social life to these first, faltering, efforts to escape from the nasty, brutish, and short existence of primitive times is the fact that the earliest representatives of civilization, like the latest, have always attempted to 'size up the situation', and, to the limit of their ability, adapt themselves to the environment in which they lived. This conviction was registered in the popular imagination of the Greeks by the myth of Prometheus.

We have said that the transition from tribal society to the society of the *polis* began when certain groups of village kin-associations resolved to stand fast and unite to protect their surplus. What may have been the fate of most of these tiny leagues or federations is quite unknown, but Thucydides at least makes it clear that their efforts at common action were merely spasmodic, occurring only when a common danger presented itself of magnitude sufficient to drive them together, and interrupted frequently by internecine feuds, such as those which the Eleusinians under Eumolpus waged against Erechtheus of Athens (ii. 15). These leagues probably relied on voluntary co-operation, reinforced by the sanctions of religion. At any rate, the debris of such groupings was left all over Greece in the religious and social gatherings which survived their independence and lasted well into the historic period—as for instance in the festival of the Marathonian tetrapolis and the mysteries of Eleusis.

The evolution toward political association properly so called began with the suppression of independent village communities and leagues, or with their absorption into more stable unions, in which the relations of authority and subjection, hitherto accepted only when danger pressed, were established and maintained in both peace and war, resulting in an immense increase of wealth and power. The first example which Thucydides cites of such a union was the maritime empire of Minoan Crete; and, indeed, the movement was originally connected with the discovery and development of the art of navigation, and for many generations confined to the islands and such mainland communities as lay on the coasts. The art of navigation, when first discovered, led to an outburst of piracy analogous to those attempts to seize and hold the richer valleys, which have already been described; but with this difference, that the pirates had an immensely greater freedom of movement than the migrant land tribes, and could raid the defenceless villages of the coasts, making away with their surplus, and conveying it to their inaccessible strongholds on the islands. Thus the practice of piracy destroyed the meagre stores of capital as they were created, and greatly retarded the growth of the communities of Greece. Piracy in the days of Homer was a respectable profession (the business ethics of civilization having not yet been created), and it survived to interrupt the peaceful commerce of the Aegean until the days of the Athenian empire. To meet this menace, Minos built and organized a fleet and constituted himself the first policeman of the Seven Seas (i. 4). With this fleet he cleared the Cyclades of pirates, and for the first time in history gave security to a considerable area within the Aegean. The revenues necessary to support his fleet were levied on those communities which, for the sake of security, accepted his sway; and besides this, they provided no doubt the sums necessary to support his state, once regarded as mythical, but in recent years accepted as in some sense a reality, as a result of the excavations in Crete.

The Cretan empire was but the first of a series of powers which followed the example and practised the methods of Minos, thus establishing areas of security over different sections of the Aegean basin. Archaeology may perhaps recover the data necessary to give an impression of their glory, but their actual history is lost in the fog that obscures the dawn of European civilization. Accordingly, in speaking of them it is not permissible to go beyond the words of Thucydides, when he says (i. 8. 3) that 'after the establishment of the Minoan navy, intercommunication by sea was vastly improved. Those who dwelt by the sea acquired much more wealth, and dwelt in greater security, so that some of them even found the capital necessary to surround themselves with walls. For, in their desire for profit, the lesser communities submitted to enslavement at the hands of the greater; and the more powerful,

through their possession of capital, brought into subjection the
lesser communities. And this was the condition in which they
still found themselves when later they undertook the expedition
against Troy'. Of such imperialisms, Thucydides makes that
of Agamemnon himself an example; rationalizing the myth of
the Pelopidae (probably on the basis of the story of Alcmaeon
as told by Herodotus) and transforming the king from a hero
of romance into an organizer of power, who 'gathered his
expedition not so much by favour as by the fear which he was
able to inspire' (i. 9. 3).

Thus, scientifically speaking, the *form* of imperialism is
everywhere the same, and consists in a relation of authority
and subjection which satisfies the need which the subject feels
for protection, at the same time as it permits the master to
realize his ambition for power. Its *function*, however, lies in the
reconciliation of these quite separate and distinct interests or
rather in the possibility of their coexistence. As a matter of fact,
empires continue to exist only so long as this coexistence of
interests is maintained.

So far, there is no distinction, in form at any rate, between
the empire and the state; and those who make the state begin
in subjection to a military force, only to be transformed later
on into a relationship of co-operation, surely forget that the
formal character of the state remains, what it has always been,
a relationship of authority and subjection. This relationship is
seen no less in the legislative and judicial activity of the modern
state than in the fact that, when necessary (and sometimes when
hardly so), public authority has recourse to police and military
coercion to make its will effective. In any form of state there are
always *some* particular interests of ruler and ruled which must be
suppressed in favour of the interests which to both are, for the
time being, predominant. The most 'absolute' ruler cannot go
farther than a certain point in realizing his own wishes. 'Russia
is governed by ten thousand clerks', was a saying of the Czar
Alexander; and Paléologue,[1] reporting a conversation held in
1917 with a Russian Prince, remarks that 'obviously regicide
is the necessary corrective to autocracy. In a sense, it might

[1] *An Ambassador's Memoirs*, ii. 314.

almost be called a principle of public law'. So also with the subjects, who as individuals and groups have always submerged and still continue to submerge important private interests to their duties as citizens. When the persistent and vigorous refusal of Sinn-Fein to co-operate with Great Britain made the name 'United Kingdom' a farce, there were two alternatives open to the Imperial Government. One was to undertake the complete subjection of southern Ireland by force of arms, and the public opinion (such as it was) of the British Isles and of America made that impossible. The other was the elimination of the Free State from the Union, and that is exactly what took place. This last example shows incidentally that the form of the state remains the same, whether it be that of an 'absolute' monarchy, or that of a liberal democracy. The king-in-parliament is no more and no less sovereign than was the Russian Czar; and the 'people' of France is no less sovereign than either, for democracy is an attempt not so much to destroy sovereignty, as to obtain for the masses of the people some degree of control over the employment of sovereign power.

In function, however (still speaking from the scientific standpoint), there is or at least arises a marked distinction between the character of imperialism and that of the state. For, while empire as a rule remains satisfied with a mere coexistence of interests between ruler and ruled, the state aims at a genuine reconciliation of such interests as existed when the state began; and further it aims at a vast extension of the field of common interest. In other words, it sets itself to develop a real sense of community, so far as this is deemed by public authority essential to the life of the whole. Circumstances determine the degree to which this process goes on in different states, and also in the same state at different times. For example, when the state is engaged in a desperate war, and fighting with its back to the wall, public authority will enforce and public opinion will normally support the complete suppression of all private interests, so far as this is possible. Such was the case even in the liberalized democracy of Athens during the crises of 440 and 431 B.C.; although, in the latter case, it was not without murmur that the landed middle-class submitted to the autocratic administration of Pericles (ii. 16. 2) and to his suppression of free speech and the right of assembly (ii. 65). These occasions were, in Athens, of course most extraordinary. Normally in the later fifth century, Athens enjoyed a régime of liberty, and government relied on no power other than that of persuasion.

Compared with the developed states of Greece, the embryonic polity claimed but a few of the interests of the citizen as falling within the scope of its activity. This was due, no doubt, partly to the narrow range of interests existing within its frontiers in those primitive times, when the activity of men was concentrated almost entirely upon agriculture and cattle-raising, and commerce and industry were yet in their infancy. But it was also due, in part, to the fact that the state was as much a usurper on earth as Zeus was in heaven, and consequently there were many activities still left to the pre-existing social and religious groups, while public authority limited its intervention to the barest essentials of security, and even so, while intervening between groups, often borrowed so far as it could the dignity and trappings, as it assumed the prerogatives, of the patriarch whom it replaced.

Nevertheless, the powers which the state did assume were vast enough—so vast indeed that, while pressure of circumstances rendered the evolution of political society necessary and possible in the peculiar conditions of the Hellenic peninsula and the islands of the Aegean, the surrounding world remained in a state of barbarism, and even those peoples of Hellenic stock, who dwelt in the remoter valleys of Aetolia and Acarnania, still preserved their tribal customs until the days of Thucydides.

Where, however, the *polis* did emerge, its evolution followed, for a certain distance at least, a common line. Normally, the state began by claiming to monopolize the means of defence within a certain geographical area and, indeed, its birth dated from the moment when that claim was asserted and made effective. Thus *imperium*, which is the authority of the state over the citizen as opposed to that of the patriarch over the kin-association, has an essentially military flavour. But this does not by any means exhaust the meaning of *imperium*, even in its incipient stages. State authority not merely assumes the protection of the subject from external aggression, but it also asserts a right to suppress such internecine feuds as disturb public order within the nascent community itself. In other words, it substitutes for the vendetta of family and clan a rudimentary system of public criminal law, the first step towards which was probably in the Greek states, as in Rome, the establishment of law and procedure governing treason. Arbitral intervention in private disputes, if it did not accompany, at any rate followed the suppression of the vendetta. But as Thucydides' interest lies mainly in the development of public law, he passes over this without comment, and merely notes (i. 5) the disarmament of the citizen and his subjection to the coercive power of the state, in contrast with the primitive conditions still in his day surviving among barbarians. However, it is clear from what he says (i. 6), that the transition to state-justice marched hand in hand with the rise of the military power. And as the vendetta was generally condemned as suicidal by Greek public opinion,[1] it is apparent that up to this point at least, political society was a distinct improvement upon what had preceded it, and that specific welfare accompanied and depended upon that organization of power.

If, scientifically speaking, it is correct to make the type of state depend upon the number and variety of interests which public authority recognizes and seeks to serve, the scientific classification of states will depend upon (a) the degree to which, normally, in any community interests are felt and held in common (function), and (b) the means adopted to give expression to those common interests (form). In all cases, Thucydides implies, there is a minimum necessary to distinguish the state on the one hand from the tribe or nation, and on the other from a mere imperialism. State and empire are differentiated from the nation in so far as the real or imaginary tie of blood which constitutes the governing principle of the latter is superseded in both by a new relationship of authority and subjection through which both masters and subjects are enabled to realize, if not common interests, at least interests which they hold con-

[1] e.g. Aeschylus, *Eumenides*.

5 per cent. of their annual income, they managed their city excellently, at the same time conducting their wars and carrying on their religious festivals.' On the other hand, tyrannies normally fell (i. 17) because of an inherent tendency to consider their own selfish and family interests to the detriment of the common welfare, and their refusal to 'live dangerously', so that on the whole 'there was nothing achieved by them worthy of account'. From this general stricture, the tyrants of Sicily were exempted, as being the recognized saviours of Hellenism in the West.

The peculiar constitution of Sparta, which saved the land-holding Dorian aristocracy, but at the cost of arresting fusion with the conquered, by which a genuine consolidation might have been attained, always excited the greatest attention and interest in Greece. Plutarch (*Lycurgus*) admires Sparta, because she alone of all Greek states, deliberately set out to 'moralize politics, and socialize morals', and the result was a realization of the Kingdom of God as Lycurgus (or whoever was the author of her institutions) saw it. In his argument and conclusion, Plutarch merely followed Plato, who regarded Sparta as the nearest earthly counterpart to the ideal state. Aristotle, while condemning Spartan communism, was nevertheless impressed by the Spartan ethos, although Herodotus had long since pointed to its weakness, when he said that 'the Spartans, once they go abroad, respect neither the laws of God nor of man'. Thucydides, however, viewing Lycurgan institutions with scientific detachment, allows himself to be neither blind to their weakness nor dazzled by their strength. Sparta interests him (i. 18) because of her peculiar survival value. For four hundred years she had been exempt from internal strife and had always been free from tyrants, thus defying, as it were, the 'law' of cyclical evolution. The stability of her institutions had given her a considerable measure of power, sufficient to enable her to exploit two-fifths of the Peloponnese, and dominate the rest, besides exercising considerable influence upon the affairs of Greece as a whole. This, in spite of the quite 'inorganic' character of her relations with the helots, which were based on terrorism and maintained by periodic butchery (iv. 80. 4). Yet

Thucydides saw that, in the face of the problem of Greek unity, Sparta was incapable of making the necessary adaptations. 'Your institutions are incompatible with those of other states' (i. 77. 6). Union had been required to meet the menace of Persia in 480 B.C., but Sparta, nominally the first power in Greece, had failed to give the necessary leadership at that time. Thus, so far as Sparta was concerned, the Persian might have come to the very borders of Peloponnese, without anything worthy of mention being done to stop him (i. 69. 5). After the wave of invasion was rolled back, when it was necessary to form an alliance to redeem the coastland of Ionia and to protect the enslaved brethren from further aggression, Sparta had withdrawn to her inglorious isolation, preferring the loss of power to risking the lives and characters of her citizens. In 431 B.C. she was already an anomaly in Greece and her institutions were obsolete. Into the mouth of her aged king Archidamus, Thucydides puts a searching prognosis of her weakness in the face of Athenian might, a prognosis which serves to heighten and intensify the criticism which her leading ally, Corinth, had already levelled against her. Thus, while Plato blindly worshipped an idol already in his day fallen, Thucydides turned with contempt from that idol which, while it still stood, had, as he well realized, feet of clay. He probably died while the Spartans were still enjoying their ignoble victory, purchased by Persian gold, but his estimate of Sparta was none the less correct, for within a generation of Aegospotami, the battle of Leuctra sounded the knell of her glory and power for ever. Thus history came to the rescue of science, confirming by the event the prognosis which science had made of Sparta.

In speaking of Sparta as 'inorganic', we consciously used a metaphor, meaning thereby to emphasize the fact that there never arose in Lacedaemon a genuine fusion of interests and sentiments among the inhabitants, but that the peers treated all other elements in the community as political outcasts, and governed them by the strong hand. Aristotle notes that, even within the circle of peers, fusion of interests, far-reaching as it was in intent, was far from being realized in fact at any time. So force was employed on more than one historic occasion to suppress recalcitrant aristocrats; and it was particularly necessary in handling the military executives—kings like Cleomenes and regents like Pausanias—both of whom perished under a cloud.

This raises the question whether political society can ever possess truly 'organic' character, or, in other words, whether compulsion can ever be completely eliminated from the body politic. For this is what political thinkers really mean when they designate the state as an 'organism'. The efforts of philosophers like Rousseau to associate the insociables, liberty and authority, making the latter depend on the former, have led to endless sophistry and have in all ages been the weapon of that brand of tyranny which delights in 'forcing the subject to be free'. To the mind of Thucydides, of course, the question does not present itself in quite this way. The only organism known to him was the organism known to science, and so, as applied to society, the word would have been a metaphor, and, strictly speaking, 'mythical' in his sense of the word. Thucydides thought rather of political society as a 'consolidation' of individuals which, although it was not literally an enlargement of the family, shared, as we have seen, something of the characteristics of the household unit. For in the household the element of compulsion at least resides in the background, and common interests and sentiments largely dominate the life and activity of the free subjects of patriarchal rule.

Accordingly, in contrast with the system of force and authority as exhibited by Sparta, Thucydides offers in Periclean Athens the picture of an alternative system which, in almost every essential, appears as the exact reverse of Lycurgan institutions. The contrast is drawn at length in the Corinthian address at Sparta, and in the consequent apologia of the Athenian delegation (i. 68–71 and 73–7); but the point that emerges above all others is that in Athens there existed a system in which it was recognized that the condition of power is consent; consent itself, in turn, being conditioned by services rendered, in the first instance to the people themselves—which is democracy, and in the second to the wider Hellenism—which is the empire.

The analysis of Athenian institutions contained in the

Funeral Speech (ii. 35–46) is full of interest from several points of view. In the first place, it is an excellent illustration of the scientific spirit which relates character to environment. Again, it illustrates the scientific method of classification by form and function. 'Athens', says Thucydides (37. 1), 'bears the name of democracy because it is organized in the interests not of the few but of the many.' Finally, the speech analyses the fruits of democracy; illustrating the power and limitations of government based on consent, that is, of government which draws its strength not merely from the formal endorsation of periodic popular elections, but also, and perhaps more intimately, from the constant endeavour to lay the cards on the table, and obtain through speech and propaganda the consent of the governed to those policies which it initiates and tries to put into effect. Of this method of government, the *Funeral Speech* itself is an excellent example. It is ostensibly a piece of war propaganda, and the argument takes the form of an appeal to the Athenians to defend the unique advantages which, through their polity, they enjoy.

Among these advantages, the purely political ideas claim first attention. In connexion with these, the speaker claims that Athens has reconciled the principle of legal equality with the claims of distinction, not indeed of wealth, but rather of character and capacity for public service. She was thus in a position to employ her stock of talent to the last available ounce. The next point emphasized is the liberal atmosphere of social life. The author of the article on Plato in *Encyclopedia Britannica*[1] observes that 'the idea of toleration in the modern sense was never distinctly present to the mind of any ancient philosopher'. If that be the case, Pericles (or Thucydides) is excluded from the ranks of ancient philosophers; since in claiming for the individual not merely the right to do what he likes (εἰ καθ' ἡδονήν τι δρᾷ—genuine liberty in the only intelligible sense of the word) but also to do so without subjecting himself to any legal penalties (ἀζημίους), or social disapproval (δι' ὀργῆς τὸν πέλας κ.τ.λ.), the speaker actually reaches the high-water mark of the theory of toleration as enunciated by John Stuart Mill.

[1] Eleventh edition, vol. xxi, p. 824.

Pericles, at the beginning of his career, had destroyed the Areopagus, thus freeing the state from the control of a body which claimed to enforce by legal measures a divine control over political life. At the time when the controversy was raging over this secularization of the state, the poet Aeschylus[1] had voiced the fears of conservatives that the elimination of authority would involve the disruption of society. Plato, writing after the event, and in view of the catastrophe which had overwhelmed the secularized and liberalized state, endorsed the Aeschylean argument that Athens' greatness depended upon the preservation of religious authority,[2] and that her decay coincided with the beginning of liberalism. In 431 B.C. Pericles could still, with some show of reason, maintain that the utmost freedom in social life was none the less compatible with complete attention to public duty (37. 3 and 40. 2). This sense of public obligation he attributed not to the fear of authority, but to a naturally healthy public spirit which exhibited itself in respect for law, hatred of oppression, and a sense of restraint.[3]

The question remains: how are such admirable qualities created and maintained? Or, in other words, what merely human (as opposed to divine) foundations are adequate to support the splendid structure of political life? The answer of Pericles is so plausible as to beguile all but the most rigid of religious bigots; it is this—we make the state worth living in and for. Economically and socially Athens is self-sufficing (αὐταρκής), but in a sense new and strange to the narrow philosophers of the exclusive city state. 'Because of the greatness of our market, the products of the whole earth are laid at our door, and we consume the products of foreign shores with as intimate an enjoyment (οἰκειοτέρᾳ τῇ ἀπολαύσει) as though they were produced in the valley of the Ilissus. Furthermore, we surround ourselves with all possible amenities of life, in the shape not merely of public festivals and amusements, but attractive private entertainments, so that by constant delights from day to day we evade boredom whether we are rich or poor.

---

[1] *Eumenides*, l. 517 ff.
[2] *Laws*, iii. 698b δεσπότις ἐνῆν τις and 700–1 αἰδώς.
[3] αἰσχύνη in the sense of σωφροσύνη.

Nor (39) do we kill joy by excluding interesting and amusing visitors, or by inflicting upon our people a grinding parade-ground discipline, which while it may serve to produce good fighting machines, is more than counterbalanced by the high spirit (εὐψυχία) with which our happy warriors take the field. Finally (40), we indulge freely in the pleasures of art and litera-ture as well as of philosophy, without in the slightest degree running into extravagance or suffering degeneracy. In conse-quence of this, Athens sets the pace for Greece, and versatility and adaptability are the special and unique marks of an Athenian in any situation in which he may be found' (41).

Thus does the speaker endeavour to establish his claim that Athens stands for something entirely original in the history of Greece and of the world,[1] and indeed worthy to serve as a model for other states. He has in fact enunciated for all time the project of a commonwealth founded on individualistic and liberal principles—the provision of well-being and satisfaction for its members. There is, however, one problem, and that the most critical, which he has still to face, and it is interesting to notice how he does so. Easy as it must have been to live for a city such as Athens, it was a different matter when it came to facing death on her behalf.

The problem of courage and self-devotion was one which excited great attention among the Greeks, and Plato's answers to them in the *Laches* and the *Crito* are of course familiar. It is interesting to observe the contrast between the arguments of Plato and the views expressed in the *Funeral Speech*. Why have these youths been willing to die for Athens, and why will others in all probability be willing to do the same in their turn? Because it is *natural* that they should be so, in keeping with their stock and their heritage.[2] It should be observed that this is represented only as a probability (εἰκός) which, like all things human, holds good only in the main, and so long as the ethos or peculiar atmosphere of Athenian life is conserved (43. 1).

---

[1] 37. I. χρώμεθα γὰρ πολιτείᾳ οὐ ζηλούσῃ τοὺς τῶν πέλας νόμους.

[2] 41. 5 περὶ τοιαύτης οὖν πόλεως οἵδε τε γενναίως δικαιοῦντες μὴ ἀφαιρεθῆναι αὐτὴν μαχόμενοι ἐτελεύτησαν, καὶ τῶν λειπομένων πάντα τινὰ εἰκὸς ἐθέλειν ὑπὲρ αὐτῆς κάμνειν.

In that case, however, the probability is so great as to amount
to a reasonable assurance. Asia, Hippocrates had said, is a vast
country and in it the gulf between government and governed
is great. You cannot expect men to risk their lives and fortunes
on behalf of despots whose interests are not their interests, and
whose wars are not their wars. Athens, however, was small,
and great only in the beauties and satisfactions which she offered
to her people. 'Gaze on the city', says Pericles, 'from day to
day; consider her might, until you fall in love with her, and when
at last her greatness has penetrated to your marrow, reflect
that her citizens have acquired all these advantages by their
daring, by their wit, and by the self-control which they have
maintained in their conduct. If you do so, you will then be
willing, in the hour of trouble and disaster, rather than submit
to be deprived of her, to make on her behalf the supreme
contribution.'[1] In these burning words are recorded the principles to which men must always turn when religious sentiment
is weak, or non-existent. They reveal the arcana of the naturalistic and humanistic state. 'Utilitarian' motives are in the last
resort lost to sight, and love of country is assimilated to the
love which men feel for their wives, or for their nearest and
dearest friends.

It is possible that intensely concrete and local patriotism may
have existed in the Athens of Pericles to a degree inconceivable
to members of the modern state, always, by comparison with the
polis, vast in extent and normally possessing a government
which is at least aloof, if it is not sometimes oppressive. It is
probable that such a patriotism may have flamed forth for a
brief period under the inspiration of Athens' great demagogue.
Actually, however, the maintenance of conditions necessary to
keep the flame alight must have been a most delicate and difficult
task, even with Pericles in control of the administration (ii. 65).
He was, says Thucydides, misunderstood and distrusted when
the plan of campaign failed; and he probably realized at the
last that his scheme of life for Athens was destined to perish
with him. In a sense, the whole sequel of Thucydides' work
is a criticism of the claim that a stable society can be erected on

[1] 43. 1 ἐραστὰς γιγνομένους αὐτῆς . . . κάλλιστον δὲ ἔρανον αὐτῇ προϊέμενοι.

the plan of the great democratic architect. The first disillusion-
ment came with the plague, as a consequence of which moral
anarchy ran riot in Athens. The next came with the Sicilian
expedition, which demonstrated that Periclean high spirit was
no match for Spartan discipline, for the Athenian troops refused
to obey orders and were driven from the field a terror-stricken
mob. But the final blow came with the malignant influence of
Alcibiades, in whose perverted brain the tender sentiment of
patriotism[1] was transmuted into a kind of political sadism,
unparalleled in any age. 'A man', says Alcibiades (vi. 92. 4),
'who has unjustly suffered the loss of his native country, should
not shrink from action. He should endeavour by every means
in his power to satisfy his desires by recovering possession of
her. This is genuine patriotism.' Pericles had compared the
sentiment of patriotism to the tender affection which a man
feels for his beloved one. The exaggerated egotism of his
nephew, baulked in his desire for possession, brutally beat and
all but murdered the alleged object of his affection.

In spite, however, of the melancholy results which followed
the death of the greatest of all demagogues, Thucydides fully
endorses the claims which Pericles had made for Athens. The
failure of Athens he ascribes to the fact that she relapsed from
Periclean principles (ii. 65), and that she never bred a second
Pericles to take the lamp from the hand of the first. But as
for Pericles himself, he had made no mistake in his estimate
of the forces which she possessed in opposition to those of the
enemy. He had, in fact, correctly 'prognosticated her power'.

[1] vi. 92. 2 φιλόπολίς ποτε δοκῶν εἶναι.

V
INTER-STATE RELATIONS

IN the view of Thucydides, the evolution of Greek society was far from being exhausted by the rise of the autonomous city state. Alone among contemporary political thinkers, he estimated correctly the overwhelming strength, both actual and potential, of those forces on the fringes of the Greek world, which made necessary a further and more thoroughgoing organization of power, if the city state itself was to survive and its economic and spiritual gains were to be conserved. The theme of Herodotus had been the successful resistance of Greece against the menace of Persian invasion, and that theme of course involved an attempt to answer the question: how came it, after all, that Xerxes was defeated? To this question, the answer given by Herodotus was vague and uncertain, and it must have been profoundly unsatisfactory to the scientific inquirer.

The pages of Herodotus reveal, indeed, a condition of affairs in Greece that was little short of ghastly. Apart from the co-operating continental states, there were the Asiatic Greeks, craven-hearted descendants of the ancient Hellenic colonists, who, whether reluctantly or not, supplied a division of that armada with which the Great King hoped to subdue their motherland. The reputed gallantry of Artemisia does not suffice to counterbalance the fact that, in the great naval battle for Greek freedom, she was fighting on the wrong side. In the ranks of the royal army there marched a group of traitors drawn from the continental states themselves. Among these were found the ignoble figure of Hippias,[1] anxious to recover by Persian help that ascendancy in Athens which his own qualities had failed to maintain, and the Aleuadae of Thessaly, who were willing to subject their country to slavery that they might become its overlords (Hdt. vii. 130. 3 and foll.). But

[1] According to one tradition. At least it is fairly clear that he was present in the Persian ranks at Marathon.

of the lot, perhaps the worst, because the most prominent in the Herodotean narrative, was Demaratus, the exiled king of Sparta. If this man's morals had been as good as his moralizings, he would never have condescended to play the part of flunkey and confidant to the Great King, who relied on him to reveal the secrets of Spartan weakness in maturing his plans for the conquest of the peninsula (vii. 101–4, and especially 234–5). Herodotus, with his eye fixed constantly on the dramatic, seems hardly conscious that there was anything improper or unworthy in the position of these men.

In his account of the campaigns (vii–ix) generally, Herodotus also reveals his complete absorption by the spectacular. He paints a glowing picture of the gallantry of Leonidas and his band; but he obscures the disgraceful truth that the heroes of Thermopylae were made the victims of a sacrifice, not so much to Persian might as to the fear and vacillation of their own countrymen, who failed to give them the support which they had undertaken to send. To Themistocles and to the wiles by which he broke the power of the Persian armada at Salamis, he pays a grudging tribute; but he represents the engagement as little more than a fortunate accident, redeemed though it was by the gallantry of the Greek contingents who shared the victory, and by the loyalty and devotion of the Athenians who made it possible. He notes, without surprise or comment, the crass selfishness which prompted the Thessalians to go over to the king the moment the imperial forces crossed their frontier, and which led the Locrians to support the cause of freedom because their neighbours, the Phocians, preferred that of slavery. The narrow particularism of Sparta, the unquestioned Medism of Argos, the neutrality of Crete, the treachery of Corcyra which promised help and then deliberately refrained from sending it, as well as the selfishness of Gelo (who had, it is true, pressing problems of his own on hand), all these points Herodotus notes with interest, but without any obvious dismay.

For, despite the vacillation of Delphi, the Greek gods, like the Greek people, were obviously on the side of freedom. When the storm threatened to break, Apollo (or his priests) might sweat black blood, and shake with terror like dice in a box, as,

in the first oracle to Athens, he himself confessed they did
(vii. 140); and he might, in the second oracle (vii. 141), state
the adamantine decree of Zeus, that all else within the borders
of Attica would be given to destruction, and the wooden wall
alone survive. But even Apollo, at last, plucked up courage,
and advised his questioners to pray to the winds. Boreas
responded to their frantic appeals with a blast (or a series of
blasts) that reduced the Persian armada to a size commensurate
with that of the allied Greeks. Above all, the Nemesis of Zeus,
who resents unwonted grandeur, busied herself with propaganda (in the shape of a dream) necessary to impel the king of
kings to his inevitable doom. Thus ultimately it was the mercy
of providence which was the ruin of Xerxes, and the salvation
of the Greeks. Such is the 'philosophic' answer which the
'philosophic' historian rendered to the question propounded by
the great war.

But to the realist, as has been said, such an answer must have
been anything but reassuring. It is not certain whether Thucydides lived to see the Great King triumphantly re-enter the cities
of Ionia, to present them with a tax bill covering arrears for the
seventy odd years which had elapsed since the formation of the
Delian confederacy. It is clear that, already after the Sicilian
disaster, his agents and himself reasserted to some purpose their
interest in Greek politics, and, by prostituting to their ambitions
in turn the military science of Sparta and the naval skill of
Athens, achieved that predominance in Greek affairs which they
had never been able to win by the sword. And to Thucydides,
it was beyond question that if, in the interval between the
victory of Salamis and the disaster at Syracuse, security and
a measure of freedom had reigned on the shores of the Aegean,
those advantages had been maintained by Athens and the
Athenian empire. It was, then, rather as a Greek patriot than
as an Athenian democrat that he praised the foresight of
Themistocles and admired the organizing genius of Pericles,
his successor. For he knew that Persian imperialism was a
menace which, though scotched, had not been killed, and he
saw no way to combat it except by its own weapons.

But the menace to Hellenism was by no means confined

to the east. Thucydides was familiar with that northland, from which within the next two generations there was destined to sweep the flame that consumed the liberties of Greece. Herodotus, in his amiable way, had given a good deal of 'copy' to Alexander of Macedon. He had enlarged on the Argive descent, and on the philhellenic proclivities of the emissary whom Mardonius used in his vigorous attempt to detach Athens and the Athenian navy from the Greek cause. Thucydides knew better; he saw, in the ambition of Alexander's successor Perdiccas, a force capable, under favourable conditions, of loosening the precarious hold which Hellenism possessed over the timber and mineral resources of the north, and sweeping the puny Greek colonies of Chalcidice and the Thrace-ward region into the sea. That force was as yet still in embryo and, to bring out its full potentialities, there was needed a fresh organization of power such as in the next century it received through the genius of Philip. But the factors were all present, and were revealed to observant students on the occasion of Brasidas' famous raid on Amphipolis.

Amphipolis, or Nine Ways, was, as he tells us (iv. 102), and as its very name would suggest, the key to control of the North Shore. After his flight from Persia (497 B.C.), Aristagoras of Miletus had attempted to found a colony on the site, but had been driven out by the Edones, who doubtless resented the prospect of being exploited by that wily adventurer. Thirty-two years later, the Athenians, at that moment disputing with the Thasians control of the mines and markets of the mainland, sent an enormous mixed colony of 10,000 settlers to the Strymon, only to be destroyed by a coalition of all the native tribes,[1] when they tried to penetrate to the interior. A third attempt at colonization under Hagnon (about 436 B.C.) was finally successful. This time the Thracian tribes failed apparently to present a united front. The Edones were driven out, and the colonizing expedition, proceeding from Eion, the Athenian depot at the mouth of the river, advanced about four miles into the interior and founded a strongly fortified post, at a bend of the Strymon, which, because it was protected by the almost

---

[1] i. 100. 3 τῶν Θρᾳκῶν ξυμπάντων.

encircling river, they designated by the name Amphipolis. This colony was of critical importance to them for three reasons (iv. 108). It gave them control of the timber lands necessary for their shipbuilding; it enabled them to exploit the mineral wealth of Mt. Pangaeus; and it protected the whole area east of the Strymon from the possibility of Spartan attack by land, which was always a danger if the Thessalians allowed the Spartans a passage through their territory.

Even in Amphipolis the population must have been exceedingly impure and, as for the promontory of Chalcidice, its inhabitants were a mixed lot of bilingual barbarians, settled alongside immigrant Greeks in little towns around the coast. The character of the population, therefore, afforded little assurance that the peninsula would stand fast for Hellenism, and there was still less reason to suppose that it would fight for Athens, the tyrant city. Accordingly, except for the vigilance of the Athenian garrisons in the larger towns, the hold which the empire possessed over the whole northland was precarious to the last degree.

Brasidas might therefore win a cheap triumph throughout the country by offering freedom and autonomy to the communities of the north, but the individual most likely to profit in the long run from the distractions of Hellenism was the Macedonian king. Perdiccas accompanied the tiny Spartan army on its marches, and assisted their general in expelling pro-Athenian parties from the towns. Athens, as Thucydides states (iv. 128. 5), was his real enemy and, if the king had been able to control his passions, he might have continued to play the Spartans against the Athenians ; but with the pettishness of a barbarian he presently conceived a spite against Brasidas and, disregarding his own best interests (iv. 128), took steps to get rid of the Spartans and make peace with the Athenians. Thus nothing stood in the way of a collapse of Hellenism in this district, except the moral deficiencies of the king.

There is nothing more striking in the political thought of Greeks (and Romans) than their attitude to the vague and terrible menace of the barbarian hinterland. In early times, the terrified imagination of the Greeks had peopled the gloomy north with monsters, at the same time as their greed pictured the boundless wealth that was supposed to exist in that unknown land. Their descendants, in the period of enlightenment, had sought to pierce the darkness that prevented a just estimate of the forces imprisoned in the lofty mountains and endless plains of Europe. Thus, for example, Herodotus gathers and reports every scrap of available evidence, whether probable or improbable, regarding the Scythians (iv. 99–117). He comments on their origin, their ethnology, and the meaning of their name. He describes their nomadic life, their customs, and their political institutions, as well as the terrible raids which, both in prehistoric and historic times, had carried them down into the Mediterranean or across the land bridge into the heart of Asia. He follows with vivid interest the Scythian expedition of Darius (iv. 118–44), which was the first attempt to penetrate the mystery of the north (118 and foll.), and he comments in characteristic fashion upon its purpose and its ignominious failure. The motives which he ascribes to the king are typical: (a) (iii. 134) that general law of expansion which compels empires to grow until they topple over and fall of their own weight; and (b) (iv. and vii. 20. 2) revenge for the supposed Scythian invasion of Asia which had taken place several centuries before, when the Persian empire itself was still unborn. Both of these motives obviously fail to explain. The former is metaphysical, the latter mythical, and neither remotely approaches the character of a 'physical' cause, such as would have satisfied the mind of Thucydides.

The vast and ill-defined region of Thrace, constituting the immediate hinterland of the Greek settlements from the Strymon to the Danube, also formed, with its inhabitants, the subject of observation on the part of Herodotus (v. 3–16). Because of his misconception of the course of the Danube, he exaggerates the size of the country (v. 3. 1), and, of its vast resources, he hardly mentions more than the hemp (iv. 74) which everywhere grows wild, and is cultivated in some sections. He gives the names of nineteen tribes, which he knows in relation to the Greek colonies of the sea-board.[1] More than

[1] v. 3. 2 n., How & Wells.

this would have been impossible for him, because he was familiar only with the geography of the coast (iv. 99). The barbarous manners of the Thracian tribes are described at length, including the custom of selling children for export as slaves (v. 6), and the mysticism of the Getae, who 'believe in immortality' (iv. 93). Civilizing influences among these tribes are referred to Ionia, and connected with the account given of that quite mythical personage, Zalmoxis (iv. 94). In his account of the conquest of the country by Megabazus (v. 1-16), Herodotus pauses to offer a full-length portrait of the various peoples who bowed to the sceptre of Persia, so that his narrative, here as elsewhere, constitutes a mine of anthropological wealth, if only the gold can be separated from the ore. In one significant passage he estimates the importance of Thrace as a whole. 'The Thracian nation', he says (v. 3), 'is, after the Indian, the greatest on earth. If it were brought under the authority of a monarch, or if it were united in sentiment, it would be invincible, and in my judgment much the most powerful of all nations. But in fact such unity is impossible, and there is no means by which it may be brought about. Accordingly the Thracian peoples are weak.'

Such is the description of Thrace, and such the estimate of its potentialities in the hands of one who, while he did not lack keenness of observation, suffered from the want of a scientific method which might have enabled him to disengage the relevant facts from the mass of material which was presented to him, if he wished to form a just judgement of the power of Thrace. But this of course was not his aim, for in his hands history had not yet become a science, with a specific aim, in relation to which facts are included or excluded according to their relevance. Thus, here as elsewhere, the notion of relevancy never comes in to check or limit the effervescent enthusiasm with which he seizes upon and incorporates in his narrative all the information which curiosity may thirst for and knowledge or fancy may suggest.

The undifferentiated character of Herodotus' account of the northland stands in sharp contrast with the sober observations of Thucydides upon the same theme. Thucydides' object being

the prognosis of power, his remarks, so far as the north shore
of the Aegean is concerned, consist of a careful and accurate
description of the relations of Greek and barbarian, especially as
these relations were affected by the war. In connexion with
Macedonia, the character and policy of Perdiccas occupies his
almost exclusive attention and (ii. 100. 1–2) he notes that under
Archelaus, his successor, there was accomplished that consolidation for which Perdiccas had striven, but which he had been
unable to achieve. The same scientific spirit dictated his
references to Thrace, especially in the account which he gives
at the end of his second book. Thus, while he endeavours to
give a more accurate idea of its size (ii. 97. 1) (an attempt
limited by the fact that the country was still largely *terra
incognita* and nothing but an approximate survey was possible),
he corrects also the exaggerated opinion expressed by Herodotus, that Thrace, after India, was potentially the most
powerful nation on earth (§ 5). No country, he declares (§ 7),
whether in Europe or in Asia, could stand comparison with
a united Scythia (or Russia). His references to the timber
and mineral wealth, the exploitation of which was so essential
for Athenian imperialism, have already been noted. With
regard to the inhabitants, their character interests him in so
far as it reveals those traits of barbarism which constitute at
once the strength and weakness of uncivilized man—their
careless generosity (ii. 97), their ferocity (i. 100, ii. 29, iv. 102,
vii. 27–30), and their reluctance to exchange the impotence of
tribal freedom for the power that comes from subjection to
a territorial monarch.

All these points come up for observation in connexion with
the account which he gives of the process of consolidation, by
which the Odrysian monarchy imposed its yoke on all but the
more inaccessible hill tribes, and of the relations which this
nascent empire bore to the analogous consolidation of Macedonia, and to the Athenian empire which occupied the sea-
board of both kingdoms. He notes especially the dynasticism
which characterized their mutual relations; the marriage
alliances (ii. 101. 6) which were designed to reconcile interests
but very frequently disturbed them; the disputed successions

which threatened the uneasy head of him who wore the crown; and, above all, the philhellenism which served to keep a Sitalces friendly to Athenian imperialism, or the 'nationalism' of a Seuthes, which opposed it.

Unlike Herodotus, Thucydides indulges in no vague and general estimates regarding the menace either of Thrace or Macedonia in relation to Greece. With regard to Thrace, he is content to state (ii. 97. 3) the sum total of revenue in gold, silver, and kind, as it stood at the accession of Seuthes, the anti-Atticizing king of the Odrysians, and to describe the tribal contingents which Sitalces was able to raise for his campaign against Perdiccas. These, when fully mobilized, numbered in all not less than 150,000 men, of whom two-thirds were infantry and the remainder cavalry, including the dreaded Cossacks (ii. 96).

It is in relation to the forces of the non-Hellenic world, and in particular to those just described, that Thucydides visualized the problem of Greek unity. From notices scattered through his pages, we have thrown together a description of those forces as they existed at the time of the Peloponnesian war, and it is obvious that they were full of hazard for Hellenism. To Thucydides, therefore, Greek unity was not what it had been to Herodotus, a mere matter of sentiment (viii. 143–4), arising from common blood and language, common worships and common customs, expressing itself entirely in moral ties, and issuing merely in such co-operation as Herodotus had depicted in his account of the Persian wars. Some form of common political action had to be discovered if Hellenism was not to be submerged.

Thus (i. 1–19) Thucydides devotes a great deal of attention to different manifestations of common action on the part of the Greeks, beginning with the Trojan war, which he represents as the first great effort of a united Hellas (9–11). As has already been observed, he attributes the possibility of such an enterprise to the fear, rather than the favour, which Agamemnon was able to inspire. From evidence contained in the Homeric catalogue of ships, he endeavours to form a rough estimate of the number engaged in the expedition, which, if his method of averaging the complements of the largest and smallest vessels be accepted, turns out to be a trifle in excess of 100,000 men—no great showing, considering that it represents an effort of the whole of Greece (10. 5). The real weakness of the force, however, was due (11. 1) not so much to a deficiency in numbers as to their lack of the resources which constitute the sinews of war. Accordingly, the members of the expedition were not merely compelled to act both as oarsmen and fighters, but they possessed no organized commissariat, and, consequently, after they had landed on the plain of Troy, they had to turn to piracy and even to agriculture to obtain sustenance. Thus their efforts were dissipated, and at no time were they able to employ their full strength against the city of Priam. It was their inability to develop their potential striking power which indeed frustrated their efforts for so many years. Thus briefly does Thucydides sketch the principle that the realization of power depends upon specialization of function and division of labour, adding (12) that Greece had still to wait for many generations before these were in any measure achieved.

The same defect of organization and control which had crippled the first great national effort led to the confusion succeeding the return of the heroes, during which the spasmodic and undirected movements of peoples characteristic of the pre-Trojan period were resumed. Hellas had still to wait for the internal peace which is the condition of expansion (12. 4) and, as this was achieved first by the commercial cities of the coasts, expansion, when it did come, took the form of a race among these cities for occupation and control of the areas to be exploited. This element of competition led also to the development of a series of minor imperialisms, among the most noteworthy of which was that of Corinth (13), always (§ 5) a commercial city, as its situation on the Isthmus indicated clearly enough. To this period Thucydides refers not merely the colonization of Ionia by Athens, but that of Italy and Sicily by the Peloponnesian powers (i. 12. 4 and vi. 1–5). As competition developed, it led to clashes between the rival systems, among which he notes (15. 3) the feud between

Chalcis and Eretria, which culminated in a war of pan-Hellenic importance[1] sometime during the course of the seventh century. It was the same desire for a place in the sun that led the Athenians, many years later, to build the fleet with which they intended to crush Aegina, but which they actually used to such good purpose at Salamis and Mycale (14. 3).

Meanwhile, the purely inland states made little or no headway in the mobilization of power (15). The smaller communities maintained their independence against the greater. Such joint enterprises as occurred were undertaken on a purely co-operative and equal basis,[2] and, at most, never amounted to more than mere border disputes.

In these circumstances, there was nothing to prevent a triumphant advance of Persia to the Mediterranean sea-board. With the fall of Croesus, and the absorption of the buffer kingdom of Lydia into the empire, the Asiatic Greek cities were exposed to subjection (16) unless, like the Phocaeans, they preferred to emigrate in a body (13. 6) and try their chance of breaking the Carthaginian monopoly in the far west. Cambyses, successor of Cyrus, continued his policy, and, sweeping round the coast of Syria, entered and overthrew the ancient kingdom of Egypt. On his way, he secured the allegiance of the Phoenicians, and with it the support of the powerful Phoenician navy, by the aid of which Darius the Great finally broke the Samian empire of Polycrates, and subjected one by one the islands of the Aegean. Thus Persia entered the field as a powerful contender for control of the eastern Mediterranean, and under the aegis of Persia the Phoenicians no doubt saw a possibility of recovering the trade which they had lost since Hellas had grasped the trident. And if Aristagoras of Miletus hoped, by his flight to the Strymon, to restore his fortunes in a region beyond reach of the Great King, he was speedily undeceived; for Darius crossed the Bosporus and conducted a series of campaigns in the north, with such success that the whole coast was soon reduced to subjection as far as the frontiers of Thessaly.

[1] *Vide*, Hdt. v. 99 and How & Wells, note.
[2] i. 15. 2 ἀπὸ τῆς ἴσης.

These facts are stated with such brevity in the early chapters
of Thucydides that their full significance might easily fail to
be appreciated. But Thucydides was entitled to assume that
the facts were familiar to the educated public for whom he
wrote, if only from the graphic narrative of his predecessor.
His brief allusions occur merely in the course of a powerful
argument in which he seeks to reveal the real reason for the
weakness of Hellenism. The full import of this argument
presently emerges: 'Thus from all sides the progress of Hellas
was retarded, so that she was able to effect nothing conspicuous,
and her action was paralysed. She never acted as a unit, and her
energies were consumed in the rivalries of autonomous city
states.'[1]

To this general rule there was, of course, one conspicuous
exception, and this Thucydides proceeds to note. Sparta,
although after the Dorian conquest she had been for many years
rent with civil strife, had at last found stability and good
government in the constitution of Lycurgus. The power
developed as a result of her institutions enabled her to conquer
and hold two-fifths of Peloponnesus, and to exercise an hegemony over the rest, besides wielding as much influence over
the extra-Peloponnesian states as her strictly local interests
would allow. Thus, at the threat of Persian invasion, she was
accepted by all the co-operating states as their natural leader,
because she exceeded any of them in power.[2] How she exercised
that leadership was familiar to the world from the pages of
Herodotus, and so also was her speedy withdrawal from the
entanglements of pan-Hellenic politics, when once the tide of
invasion had been repelled. Thucydides merely notes her
reluctance to remain 'on the job' and finish the remainder of
the barbarian business (i. 75. 2), and the relief which the co-
operating Greeks experienced at the departure of their oppressive general, Pausanias (i. 95. 1). The subsequent election of
Athens to the vacant post of leader was a foregone conclusion,
in view of the strongly expressed desire of the confederates that

---

[1] i. 17 οὕτω πανταχόθεν ἡ Ἑλλὰς ἐπὶ πολὺν χρόνον κατείχετο μήτε κοινῇ φανερὸν
μηδὲν κατεργάζεσθαι, κατὰ πόλεις τε ἀτολμοτέρα εἶναι.
[2] i. 18. 2 Λακεδαιμόνιοι . . . δυνάμει προύχοντες.

she should accept it, and her own obvious qualifications for the position (i. 95 and i. 18. 2). For the strength of her navy gave her a preponderant position, comparable with that which Sparta occupied on land. Thus, while Athens herself remained a member of the Peloponnesian league till 460 B.C. and, as such, was summoned by Sparta along with other allies to lend aid during the critical Helot revolt (i. 102. 1), she was already since 477 B.C. exercising an hegemony of her own and, indeed, she was rapidly extending this hegemony over the whole Aegean basin, at the same time greatly enlarging the number of states which were directly subject and tributary to herself. It is not surprising, therefore, that Sparta feared and distrusted her powerful ally, so far indeed as to dispense with her services; but, in so doing, she committed the fatal mistake of discrediting the pro-Lacedaemonian party in Athens, and throwing the government into the hands of the democratic imperialists. The immediate consequence was the so-called First Peloponnesian War. This struggle, although mainly directed by Pericles against Corinth, with the object, no doubt, of obtaining for Athens a foothold in the area of exploitation north-west of the Corinthian gulf, soon expanded into a general war, in which for the first time in Greek history a first-class power sought to establish a land empire in the Peninsula. But Athens' far-flung imperial interests nullified her design, and the war, though full of humiliation for Sparta, was finally brought to an end by the peace of 445 B.C.[1]

Despite the silence of Thucydides on the subject, it is probable that this peace, which aimed to establish a *modus vivendi* for Hellas, had been preceded, three years before, by a similar arrangement between Athens and the Persian empire. The so-called Peace of Callias, in 448 B.C., appears to have brought to an end the protracted conflict between East and West, by recognizing Athenian claims to dominate the Aegean basin and the Greek cities along the Asiatic coast as far as the eastern boundary of Lycia. The Athenians on their part undertook to abandon their more ambitious scheme of interference with Persian rights in Cyprus and Egypt, in exchange for the

[1] e. g. in the matter of transplanting the rebel Helots to Naupactus.

privilege of trading freely within the borders of the empire. If this was the case, the Peace of Callias marks a distinct advance in the relations between Greek and Barbarian. The treaty, if it was actually made, was probably sanctioned by the usual oaths, sworn by each of the contracting parties in the name of their own gods. Its real significance, however, was that it marked the triumph of humanistic principles in public international law. Greeks and Persians had evidently resolved to face their problems boldly, and bring to an end a conflict that had degenerated into a senseless and wasteful expenditure of blood and treasure. Accordingly, both sides compromised their more extravagant claims, and agreed to an arrangement which secured the real interests of each, in direct relation to their power to uphold and develop those interests. Thus the humanism of the fifth century threw overboard the ancient notion that East and West were inevitably involved in eternal conflict; and this superstition, like the so-called law of imperial expansion, ceased to dominate the minds and determine the actions of men.

From the standpoint of Greek inter-state relations, the Peace of 445 B.C. constituted a similar landmark in the evolution of Hellenism, and is the real turning-point in the history of the fifth century.[1] It marks, indeed, the death of the principle of the autonomous, self-sufficing city state. The vital need of inter-state co-operation, in one form or another, was now at last appreciated, and Hellenism apparently resolved to pool its resources and risk its fortunes in one of the two great existing systems—the Peloponnesian league or the Athenian empire. While the selfishness of states like Corcyra, or the insignificance of those like Melos, might for some years keep them autonomous, provision was made in the treaty that such independent communities might enrol in whichever of the two great federations they preferred, and in the meanwhile they remained anomalies in the new world created by that settlement. The expected happened and, by the beginning of the Peloponnesian war, or at any rate during the course of the struggle, practically all the Greek states, as well as the greater part of the barbarian

[1] Rather than the transfer of the treasury from Delos to Athens.

world, were drawn into the orbit of Greek inter-state politics,[1] so that the contest became in effect a world war. This, no doubt, is why Thucydides regarded it as having a more profound significance for human history than even the Persian wars (i. 23. 1–3), the greatest which Hellenism had hitherto experienced.

The settlement of 445 B.C., recognizing as it did the necessary implication of developments in the Greek world since the Persian invasions, was apparently accepted on all sides with a certain degree of equanimity. By no single power, however, was the treaty hailed with greater satisfaction than by Corinth, who saw in the clause permitting states to punish their rebellious allies, the legal recognition of her time-honoured claim to discipline her own insubordinate colonies, especially Corcyra. Accordingly, in the hour of Athens' greatest difficulty and distress, during the great rebellion of 440 B.C., Corinth steadily resisted the temptation to take advantage of Athenian embarrassments. While Sparta yielded to the appeal of the rebels, and actually dispatched a force into Attica with the intention of dealing her great rival a body blow, Corinth stood firm in her insistence that Athens should be allowed a free hand within her own confederacy, and she was the means of preventing the forces of the Peloponnesian league from being brought to bear against Athens in that great emergency.

It is improbable, however, that Sparta had given more than a reluctant assent to the treaty which, as she saw, afforded legal recognition to the Athenian empire, and paved the way for that immense consolidation of resources which made Athens, despite the loss of some of her tribute, a greater force than ever in the Greek world (i. 80–5 and ii. 11–13). In 440 B.C. Sparta had shown herself willing to throw her weight in the scale, in order to reverse the settlement made only five years before; and again, in 431 B.C., she professedly took the field in defence of the principle of autonomy. It was in vain that Pericles directed attention to the insincerity of Sparta in championing such a principle (i. 144. 2). Vigorous and oppressive as was her

---

[1] i. 1. 2 κίνησις γὰρ αὕτη μεγίστη δὴ τοῖς Ἕλλησιν ἐγένετο καὶ μέρει τινὶ τῶν βαρβάρων, ὡς δὲ εἰπεῖν καὶ ἐπὶ πλεῖστον ἀνθρώπων.

own imperialism within the limited range of its application,
beyond that point the interests of Sparta clearly demanded that
there should be no great consolidation of resources, such as
that represented in the Athenian empire. The mere existence
of that empire upset the balance of power as it had been
maintained by Sparta during the later sixth and early fifth
centuries, and constituted a standing menace to the 'liberties'
of Hellas. Almost invulnerable against attack by land, Athens
possessed through her command of the sea offensive force of
immense weight and range (i. 80–5, 140–4), a power the full
significance of which Athenians themselves hardly realized,
until it was revealed to them by Pericles, in his speech of
encouragement (ii. 60–4). It is not surprising, therefore, that
the oligarchical elements in the states of Greece were almost
unanimous in their hatred and fear of the tyrant city (ii. 8. 4).
Many of them had already felt the weight of her strong arm,
and those who had not done so shared, no doubt, the gloomy
forebodings of danger which the Mytileneans expressed on the
eve of their unsuccessful revolt (iii. 9–14). We observed that
the treaty of 445 B.C. marked the death of the autonomous,
self-sufficing city state. It would be truer to say that the conception of autonomy, although legally subverted by that
settlement, survived in fact in Sparta, the focus of reaction,
and also among the aristocratic elements throughout the Greek
world whose spiritual home was Lacedaemon. At any rate, it
still possessed enough vitality to serve as the rallying cry of
all those who yearned to reverse the decision of the fifth
century, and reduce Hellas once more to the impotent position
which she had occupied at the time of the Persian invasions.

By the terms of settlement in 445 B.C., the Hellenic world was
regarded as falling into two great spheres of influence, within
each of which the dominant powers were to enjoy freedom in
arranging internal disputes. With regard, however, to such
causes of friction as might arise between the two competing
systems, or individual members thereof, the treaty sought to
pave the way for a general method of settlement, by providing
that such disputes should in all cases be submitted to arbitration
before a court which should be mutually agreed upon as

acceptable to both parties. Thus, in another respect, the treaty constituted a landmark in the evolution of Greek civilization, for it appears to have embodied the first general arbitration pact in the history of Europe. Even states which for the time being remained outside the limits within which formal co-operation had been pledged, found it politic to offer arbitration of outstanding grievances, and Corcyra actually did so in her dispute with Corinth regarding their conflicting claims to control the colony Epidamnus (i. 28. 2). The offer, in the case of Corcyra, must have been purely voluntary. But, as between signatories of the treaty, such arbitration was compulsory, if the instrument itself was to remain valid. Accordingly, while Sparta and the Peloponnesians, ignoring that clause of the treaty, voted (i. 88) that Athens had violated in other particulars the pledges embodied in that settlement, and that a *casus belli* existed, Athens, on her part, was in a position both to declare (i. 140. 2) that she had offered to arbitrate all outstanding grievances, and to complain that the Peloponnesians had not done so, but had preferred the arbitrament of the sword. In this contention she appears to have been perfectly correct, as the Spartans themselves admitted after the conclusion of the Archidamian war, in attributing the unsatisfactory issue of that struggle to the fact that they had entered it in flagrant violation of their oaths and of their solemnly pledged word (vii. 18. 2).

Thus, the march of events following the defeat of Xerxes had led to the division of Greece into two great systems, and these systems, unhappily, drifted into competition with each other, instead of standing together as a unit for the defence of Hellenism against the dark and sinister perils which menaced her from the outside world. Consequently, the general arbitration pact included in the treaty was of the highest importance, because it afforded a means of reconciling differences, and compromising interests where they crossed or conflicted, as they did at many points. The means adopted were, in this case, as in the case of the treaty between Athens and Persia, thoroughly in keeping with the humanistic spirit of the fifth century, and with the scientific realism of that age. Neither treaty aimed to establish a millennium; each sought merely the recognition and definition of established interests, as the necessary preliminary of mutual understanding and good will. In the case at least of the Peace of 445 B.C., this step was supplemented by the arbitration pact, which entrusted the settlement of future disagreements to the good offices of neutral parties, and was based upon the hope that a sense of common interest in their Hellenic heritage would override any difference that might arise and would make possible an arrangement by mutual consent.

Thus the negotiations preceding the outbreak of the great war turned largely, if not altogether, on the interpretation of different interests and rights as set forth by the treaty. But behind the terms of the treaty there lay all the subterranean forces, economic, moral, and spiritual, which made either for or against the unity of Hellenism. Accordingly, Thucydides devotes the major portion of his analysis to an examination of these forces, in an effort to show how a particular combination of them disrupted the unity of Hellas, and precipitated the catastrophe.

On the side of Athens these included a strong sense of assurance, not indeed in her star, but rather in the services which throughout the period following the invasions she had rendered to the Greek world. The moral offence which she had given in the enslavement of Naxos, and the threat which that and other incidents of her career implied against the spirit of autonomy, were more than counterbalanced by the striking fact that she had made the Aegean safe for Hellenism (vi. 87. 4). Irreconcilable aristocrats, both in the imperial city itself and throughout the empire, might complain of the oppression of Athenian law courts, but the real source of their irritation was that the strong arm of Athens was everywhere raised to redress the balance of centuries and safeguard the interests of the poor; and, as a matter of fact, the very liberalism of her methods in dealing with civil and criminal cases which required attention was made the cause of reproach against her (i. 73–8). Coupled with and reinforcing this sense of virtue, was the confidence of Athens that she was equal to any possible combination of forces which the Peloponnesians could level against her, and consequently, if she saw an opportunity to strengthen her position, whether in Chalcidice, in the Megarid, or in the west, there was no particular reason why she should hesitate to take advantage of this, provided that her action involved no breach of the treaty (i. 140-4).

On the other hand, the Peloponnesian league was essentially limited and local in character, revolving so to speak about Lacedaemon, and condemned by the peculiarity of its organization to a greater or lesser dependence upon Spartan military force. In the case of all the smaller agricultural and inland powers, this dependence was to all intents and purposes absolute. The local aristocracies everywhere relied for the protection of their interests upon the might of the only professional army in their midst. That army, as has well been observed,[1] was, within certain tactical limits, unrivalled in the Greek world but, as it represented first and foremost merely the military aspect of Dorian ascendancy in Lower Peloponnese, it was an army chained to its base. And as for the confederates, they were all at once workers and fighters (αὐτουργοί) and thus no more able than the Spartans themselves to spend long periods abroad in fighting, when their work on the land required them to be at home. In other words, they lacked that essential of power which Thucydides had noted as the great defect of primitive times—specialization of function—while Athens, through her professional fighting services, and the tribute which made these possible, possessed it in ample measure.

To this general dependence there was one notable exception, namely, that of the commercial and maritime oligarchy of Corinth. With imperial interests of her own to serve, Corinth, as has been said, had accepted the treaty of 445 B.C. because the treaty seemed to guarantee those interests and protect her from the dangers to which she had been exposed at the hands of the earlier Periclean imperialism during the so-called First Peloponnesian War. If in 431 B.C. she was found to be leading the forces making for war against Athens, the reason is that she regarded the intervention of Athens in the Corcyrean dispute as a revival of the menace which in 445 she had deemed to be eliminated. Consequently, the influence which only nine years

[1] Grundy, *Thucydides*.

before had been used on behalf of Athens was now thrown into the scale against her; the object of Corinth being to fight a 'limited liability' war, to vindicate her rights under the treaty as she saw them. The weakness of her position was that she proposed to allow no one to interpret those rights except herself. In other words, she violated the most important clause in the settlement which she professed to champion and defend.

Thucydides draws no moral from the failure of the treaty to save Hellenism from the horrors of the Peloponnesian war; but, if a moral is to be drawn, it is surely this. The treaty failed to hold because of the infirmity of human wisdom and human will. On all sides, men allowed their sense of common welfare to be blinded by their own partial interests, and obscured by their fears and passions. Instead, therefore, of holding fast to the procedure which humanism had dictated, and compromising such interests as they could not reconcile, they reverted to the ancient and suicidal policy of brute force, which destroys all interests, including those which it seeks to protect, and leaves all parties to share a common fate of poverty and distress.

Our present purpose is not to attempt any justification of Thucydides' statements concerning the causes of the war, nor do we wish to weary the reader by traversing once more a familiar chapter in Greek history. We desire merely to illustrate the conceptions which Thucydides, as a scientific observer, held with regard to the scope and character of international relations. But, in view of the considerations outlined above, we find it difficult to follow those commentators who reject the account of Thucydides, and search the pages of obscure and second-hand authorities to find an explanation of the conflict more plausible than his. Their difficulties, indeed, seem to have arisen largely because of their failure to formulate the question at issue in terms which would have been comprehensible to Thucydides and to most of his contemporaries. To him, the question was not one of abstract rights and wrongs, but merely of rights which had been accepted by inter-state agreement and incorporated, so to speak, into public international law. Where such rights appeared vague, so that their interpretation led to conflicting views, the treaty made provision for the solution of such conflicts, through the clause which required arbitration of differences, and it is noteworthy that Athens at least offered to arbitrate all points at issue. Subject, however, to the above limitation, the Athenian government felt no scruple whatever in advancing her interests at every possible opportunity. Thus, for example, she had accepted the Corcyrean alliance, because of the assurance which it presented of completely commanding the sea, and the hope of opening the door to increased influence in Magna Graecia. Pericles, as a prudent statesman, having in mind the interests of his country, strongly recommended the acceptance of that alliance, although he was well aware that it involved the likelihood of a rupture with Corinth. But the prospective advantages were to him sufficient to counterbalance the possibility of war; and, should war be the consequence, he had no fear of the outcome. History may condemn him on the ground that he was short-sighted in his views and mistaken in his estimates, although Thucydides himself defends him on both counts (ii. 65); but human standards cannot be found, by which he may be convicted on any other grounds than these.

That, throughout the controversies leading to war, Athens occupied what her contemporaries regarded as a strong 'moral' position, is clearly revealed by the conduct of her leading enemies, Corinth and Sparta. The Corcyrean alliance, and Athenian interference with the control which Corinth exercised over the internal affairs of Potidaea, had touched Corinthian interests at a vital point. Thereafter, fear and distrust of Athens combined to turn her into a veritable firebrand, and she never rested until she had induced Sparta and the Peloponnesians to take the law into their own hands and declare that a *casus belli* existed. In her efforts to bring about this decision, she descended to the expedient of bullying and threatening her nominal leader and allies. For Sparta, despite the fear and jealousy which had marked her attitude towards Athens ever since she had sought in vain to prevent the rebuilding of the city, destroyed in the conflict for Greek independence, was in the crisis of 431 conscious of no feeling so much as that of impotence in face of the novel military problem presented by the Athenian empire. This was certainly the feeling voiced

by her aged and experienced monarch, Archidamus, and shared
no doubt by many Spartans, for it was with some difficulty that
the leaders of the war party extracted from the reluctant
citizens a decisive vote in favour of war (i. 86–7). The same
difficulty apparently attended their efforts to secure the assent
of the league as a whole, and here again Corinth strained every
nerve to influence their decision (i. 120–4). When, however,
the war party was once in the saddle, their real purposes were
speedily disclosed. The points in dispute were one after the
other made the pretext of demands upon Athens, each one of
which was more intolerable than the last, until in a final
ultimatum, Sparta revealed her real purpose by demanding that
Athens should at once surrender her empire as the condition
of peace (i. 139. 3). Thus, by her conduct, she exposed the
utter insincerity of the profession that she desired anything
short of the complete destruction of the Athenian empire. Not
only this, but in the strange demand, put forward at the beginning of the negotiations (i. 126), that the Athenians should
'expel the curse of the goddess', she deliberately sought to
obscure the real issue, and at the same time embarrass Pericles.
In thus proposing that the sins of the fathers should be visited
on the children, she not merely attempted to divert the thoughts
of men from the points in question and from the treaty upon
which they were based but, by aligning herself with all that was
obscurantist and reactionary in the consciousness of Greece,
she sought to obtain for herself in that quarter the moral support which she could never expect to win from the enlightened
public opinion of the fifth century.

VI

THE PROBLEM OF GOVERNMENT

FROM the standpoint of science, power normally goes hand-in-hand with welfare, in the sense that different manifestations of power arise as a rule in response to certain specific needs, and exist to safeguard certain specific interests. Thus, for example, the state, which is a definite manifestation of power, arises when a number of human beings, unconnected by ties of blood and family religion, are thrown together within a given territory, and are faced with the problem of discovering a *modus vivendi* which shall be acceptable to all or at least to the bulk of the inhabitants. This is the 'consolidation' to which allusion was made in an earlier chapter. It is a process of fusion which, when successful, issues in a form of association to which Greeks and Romans gave the name of *polis* or *civitas*, thus clearly distinguishing it from the earlier 'natural' forms of association, the family, clan, and tribe or nation.

But power and welfare, though far from incompatible, are nevertheless separable both in thought and in fact. In the state, for example, there are always certain interests which are suppressed, and there are certain others which are either ignored or left to be realized by communal groups. These interests, when they are strong enough, seek expression alongside those which are established and fostered by the state, and occasionally they seek expression even at the expense of those interests, so that the existence of the state itself is imperilled. When this happens, there arises within the community what the Greeks called *stasis*.

Already, in his account of the evolution of Greek society, Thucydides had called attention to this phenomenon, which rent the nascent communities in twain and for generations retarded the development of Greece (i. 1–3). The state, as he pointed out, begins with capital; the accumulation of capital results inevitably in a distinction between rich and poor, the exploiting groups and the exploited. Hence a pronounced tendency to strife within the bosom of the community; a strife moreover which is suicidal, inasmuch as it consumes the scanty store of accumulated wealth which is the bone of contention, and exposes both factions to a common danger of extinction.

In those states which surmounted the perils of their early life, the tendency toward internal disruption had been overcome in various ways, as circumstances suggested and wisdom dictated, but the triumph in all cases was merely temporary, and eternal vigilance was the price of survival. Thus, for example, many states during the Hesiodic age of iron, when agriculture was almost the sole means of subsistence, resorted to the device of colonization as a means of eliminating that surplus of population which constantly grew and could never be assimilated. But any fresh shock, such for instance as the invention of coinage, involved the danger of upsetting the economic and political equilibrium; and, as a matter of fact, revolution and tyranny were the normal fate of all communities which exposed themselves to such shocks. Sparta alone, through the exclusive system which she adopted, and the discipline which she maintained, was able to survive the perils that attended the period of Greek expansion and, throughout the four centuries preceding the time when Thucydides wrote, she was successful in preserving her economic and political institutions intact. Not only this, but the weight of her sword was thrown into the scale against revolution and, during the latter part of the sixth century, the majority of the continental states settled down to a régime in which the landed and commercial oligarchies found support for their sway in the powerful backing of Sparta and the Peloponnesian league (i. 18–19).

This period of oligarchical supremacy was, however, destined to last for only a short time. Herodotus had described the extraordinary release of pent-up energy which in Athens had followed the expulsion of the tyrants and was the direct result of the democratic revolution under Cleisthenes (v. 66–73, and foll.; vi. 131). Hitherto in the Greek states opposition to the established order had normally followed violent courses, and issued in tyrannies. The tyrants, although they professed themselves champions of the down-trodden, and although the wiser among them sought to camouflage the true nature of their power by outward observance of constitutional forms (Thuc. vi. 54), nevertheless failed to anaesthetize their subjects for any great length of time. It was realized that their sway was illegitimate, because it represented a violent break with all that was sacred and traditional in the communal life, and also that their representation of the oppressed, whatever it might amount to, was never more than incidental to their own selfish pursuit of power. Thus they were rarely able to transmit their ascendancy to more than two generations of their successors, and Greek public opinion, feeble and undeveloped though it still was, sooner or later cast them into the rubbish heap as greedy adventurers (i. 17; vi. 53-9). The constitutional reforms of Cleisthenes, therefore, marked a significant advance in Greek political invention, inasmuch as they afforded for the first time a means of direct political self-expression to the masses of the people, and an effective method of controlling the government of the state.

Surprise and shock among the possessing classes followed this unexpected development, by which they saw their power menaced by the tyranny no longer merely of individuals, but of the majority of the people. Sparta, summoned in haste by the terrified Athenian aristocracy to undo her own work, found to her surprise and dismay that she was incapable of setting back the hands of the clock and speedily deserted the task which she was unable to accomplish. The Athenian aristocracy, however, although for the time being abandoned, was nevertheless powerful and energetic enough to offer a vigorous opposition to the new order. In the years which followed, Tory democracy, as represented by the Alcmaeonidae, appears to have been hard pressed, so much so indeed that when the exiled tyrant Hippias sought from Persia the assistance which he had failed to find in Hellas (Hdt. v. 92) the Athenian government itself endeavoured to forestall him by making an alliance with the Great King (v. 96). Rumours of Alcmaeonid intrigue with Persia were current as late as the battle of Marathon. 'It is a marvel to me, and I cannot credit the report', says Herodotus (vi. 121), 'that the Alcmaeonidae ever held up a shield to the

Persians by agreement, wishing that the Athenians should be subject to the barbarians and to Hippias.' His reasons for discrediting such rumours are perhaps not very conclusive. 'They at all times shunned and hated tyrants; by their contrivance the Peisistratidae had abandoned the tyranny; and they, rather than Harmodius and Aristogeiton, were the real liberators of Athens' (*l.c.*). Finally (124) he dismisses the theory that they betrayed their country because they had conceived some grudge against the Athenian people.

'Nevertheless, a shield was held up, and this cannot be denied, for it was so.' To us, it is not so incredible that the Alcmaeonïdae, hard pressed on all sides, and disappointed that the democracy had not afforded them the support which it at first seemed to promise, should have fallen back for protection on Persia at a time when the flame of Hellenic national consciousness still burned dimly, if at all. Nor is it astonishing that the grandson of Cleisthenes of Sicyon, and the son of Megacles of Athens, should in the end have reverted to the policy of compromising claims which he could not defend, even at the expense of making an arrangement with the son of Peisistratus.

Democracy in Athens, however, survived the obscure perils of its birth. It was an attempt to organize the interests of the 'under-dog', and to give expression to those interests through the political machinery invented by Cleisthenes, and by him superimposed on the existing constitution of classes and tribes. From its inception, therefore, it had a political character, inasmuch as it aimed to transfer the issues which divided men to a new forum, and to have them settled by the novel method of opinion rather than by the ancient method of force. The political character of the arrangements is evident in many respects, but in no particular is it more obvious than in the institution of ostracism. This quaint device may perhaps have suggested itself to Cleisthenes as a result of the unhappy experiences of his own family during their long struggle with the Peisistratidae for control of Athens, a struggle in the course of which they found themselves driven from their native land, and deprived both of citizenship and property, so that a revolution was necessary if they were ever to repossess themselves of those advantages.

Ostracism is usually described as a device intended to prevent tyranny. It was rather designed to ensure a measure of stable government by eliminating opposition leaders for a limited period; and at the same time to mitigate the bitterness of party strife through the provision that political exiles should not be dishonoured by the loss of those privileges of citizenship and property which, at any rate under ancient conditions, were as precious as life itself. A remark of Aristotle illustrates the peculiarity of the status to which ostracized citizens were subjected. In 481 B.C., he says (*Ath. Pol.* 22), 'all the ostracized persons were recalled, on account of the advance of Xerxes; and it was laid down as a rule that persons subjected to ostracism must live between Geraestus and Scyllaeum, on pain of the irrevocable loss of civic rights.' Athens reserved the right of recalling exiles to active participation in civic duty, when state requirements made this desirable or necessary. Thus, not unlike the party government of modern parliamentary states, ostracism was really intended as a cure for stasis; the method in both cases being really the same, taking the form, so to speak, of 'sublimating' antagonisms which it is impossible to suppress. It is of course recognized that modern free states have gone a long way farther in this direction than the timid Cleisthenic democracy felt itself able to do. Modern opposition leaders are rarely if ever exiled, except in a purely metaphorical sense. In fact they normally remain in Parliament to criticize the administration which, for the time being, has gained the confidence of the majority of the electorate.

Despite the faltering conduct which marked the years of its infancy, Athenian democracy was destined to a brilliant career. Herodotus, as has been noted, does scant justice to the qualities of Themistocles, the second great leader of the people. Under him, however, democracy got nothing less than a fresh lease of life when, through his wise counsel, the Athenians took to the sea. If the immediate purpose of Themistocles, in urging the construction of a navy, was that it should be utilized to crush Aegina, he must have intended to attach the growing commercial and maritime interest to the popular cause, and no doubt he succeeded in his purpose, as the ostracism of Aristeides

reveals. For Aristeides was the champion of the substantial
middle class of landed proprietors, and the latter still wore the
laurels which they had won at Marathon. A powerful combination, therefore, was needed against them to secure from the
assembly a vote sufficient to drive their leader out of public
life. There can be little doubt that this vote was obtained from
the growing commercial class, together with the masses who
constituted the proletariat, and especially those who in the
political jargon of the future were to be known as the 'sea-
faring rabble'. The bitter hatred which Themistocles aroused
by his maritime policy was not forgotten even in the hour of
his triumph against Persia; and the pages of Herodotus still
reveal the relentless spite with which his enemies sought to
minimize his achievements and discredit his character, in
death no less than in life. Yet he maintained his place in the
confidence of the people long enough to associate the cause of
democracy with that of Hellenic nationalism; and, in the brief
period allowed him, he rebuilt the city and initiated the policy
of collecting indemnities from the renegade island states. It
is therefore nothing less than the truth to designate him, as
Thucydides does, the true founder of the democratic empire;
although the task of rearing the framework of that empire was
to be entrusted to other hands. For Aristeides, whose noble
character was equalled only by his patriotism, had evidently
seen the light. Salamis had taught him and the party of which
he was the spokesman that the safety and glory of Athens
depended on the sea rather than on the land. Thenceforth, the
middle-class conservatives lent a qualified support to the
democracy, which lasted with some interruptions until after the
death of Pericles. It was from the standpoint of middle-class
conservatism that Thucydides penned the appreciation of
Pericles, which is to be found in the sixty-fifth chapter of his
second book.[1]

[1] Aristotle, *Ath. Pol.* 23 and 24, seems desirous of stealing the democratic
platform for Aristeides. The notion that, by quitting the country districts
and settling in the city, 'they would all be able to earn a living, some by
service in the army, others in the garrisons, others in the civil service'
sounds very much more like Themistocles or Pericles than it does like the
'incorruptible' leader of the Marathonomachi.

Aristotle notes (*Ath. Pol.* 25) that, during a period of about seventeen years following the Persian invasion, Athenian democracy underwent a second eclipse, until in the year 462 B.C. Ephialtes revived the popular cause. In his attack on the Areopagus the same authority states that he was assisted by Themistocles. But, as is evident from the statement of Thucydides (i. 137), Themistocles must have been already in exile in 466 B.C. Nevertheless Ephialtes, in his assault on that citadel of aristocratic power, acted in the true Themistoclean tradition, if he was not actually inspired by advice from the victim of aristocratic and Lacedaemonian intrigue (i. 135. 2). And, whether or not the bones of Themistocles were secretly conveyed to their last resting-place in the soil of Attica, in accordance with the dying patriot's request (i. 138. 6), this at least is true, that his ideas survived to blossom forth in the glory of the Periclean age.

In Pericles the democracy found its last great leader, a worthy successor not only to Themistocles but to Cleisthenes, and in his person the Alcmaeonidae resumed the task of carrying the democratic programme to its fruition. It is unfair to concentrate attention on the aesthetic and cultural achievements of the Periclean age, and to lose sight of the soil in which these fine flowers were rooted. In his own day the great demagogue was misunderstood and misrepresented by the malignity of his enemies, who saw in his highly elaborated scheme of state support merely an attempt to bribe the people with their own money, seeing that he had none of his own. A more serious count against him was that levelled by Thucydides, son of Melesias, who protested against a system which permitted Athens to deck herself like a vain woman, with the surplus of tribute that ought properly to have been restored to the allies. Pericles, too proud even to reply to the first charge, had his answer ready for the second. The *quid pro quo* which the allies received was security, and that in a measure which the Aegean had never enjoyed before. So he steadily proceeded with the consolidation of the empire, which had already begun before his time with the enslavement of Naxos, and as each rebellious state was brought to heel, he made ample provision for its future obedience, by imposing the democratic principle of government upon the citizen body. The inscriptions fully illustrate what Thucydides means when he says that 'the Athenians set up a democracy in the town'. In Erythrae, Miletus, Chalcis, and elsewhere throughout the empire, every citizen pledged fidelity in word and deed to the Athenian demos, under pain of banishment, death, and confiscation of goods,[1] and in each of these towns a liberal franchise and magistracies subject to popular control were instituted after the Athenian pattern.

Thus, while the surviving oligarchies in Greece leaned for support on Sparta and the Peloponnesian league, the Athenian empire reflected the solidarity of the democratic interest and the ascendancy of the democratic principle; and for a few years following the great rebellion (440 B.C.) a general equilibrium was attained throughout the Hellenic world.

The question may be asked: do these forms, whether oligarchic or democratic, represent what in modern terminology is called class-domination? In one sense, Thucydides would have seen no reason to reject this view. For, from the standpoint of science, Greek political parties of whatever stripe were, so to speak, rooted in the soil. That is to say, their general outlook was determined by its physical basis. In saying this we by no means wish to imply that it was, in the Marxian sense, materialistic. That doctrine is rightly rejected because it degrades history to a mere scramble for bread and jam; and because, to those who accept it, ideas are reduced to 'ideology', so that political propaganda becomes the science of 'injecting opinions' as one would the virus of a plague. From any such one-sided conclusion Thucydides escaped, because, as has already been made clear, he was free from the trammels of Aristotelian logic. For him, therefore, there were neither material nor ideal, but only physical causes; and these were the causes proper to the nature of man. In this sense there are few who will deny that political opinions are 'class' opinions, seeing that they reflect the temperament and general outlook which are the natural results of habit and education; always admitting of course that

---

[1] Hill, *Sources for Greek History*, i. 125, 126, 127, 129, 130.

in opinion, as in botany or zoology, there remains the possibility of 'sports', which suddenly and unaccountably vary from the norm.

This being the case, we find it difficult to subscribe to the view that, while in the modern state parties divide on questions of principle, Graeco-Roman political life rarely, if ever, exhibits more than a conflict of class with class. Admittedly, among oligarchies, whether of the exclusive Spartan, or of the more liberal Corinthian type, a relatively narrow circle of full citizens shared the advantages of communal life. Consequently, in such states there were few real political questions upon which a division of opinion might occur, although even these states exhibited political life, so to speak, in embryo. The discussion in Sparta, preliminary to the declaration that a *casus belli* existed with Athens, is a good illustration of what is meant. The democracies, however, exhibited a much richer and fuller and, in the genuine sense of the word, more truly 'political' life. It is the imperishable glory of Cleisthenes that he fully accepted the territorial principle, with all its implications, and that he dragged the concept of *the people* into the full light of day. Henceforth, though in Athens there continued to exist marked distinctions of class and privilege, the great masses of the population were brought within the pale of political privilege, simply in virtue of their residence on the soil of Attica. And, within the relatively wide circle of those who now enjoyed active political rights, the issues which rose to the surface were settled before the bar of what may justly be described as genuine public opinion. The same thing is true, only over a much wider area and to a much greater degree, in the Roman republic. There the territorial principle was successively victorious over the pretensions of (*a*) the patricians to dominate and exploit the plebs; (*b*) the new patricio-plebeian aristocracy to dominate the Italians; and (*c*) the Italians to dominate the provincials. Within the community also, though class distinctions were never attacked either in theory or practice, the lowest orders, even slaves, slowly but surely attained status and protection under the law. Under Pericles, Athens herself unfortunately reverted to a narrower conception of citizenship which, if it had been held earlier, would have put most of the great personalities of the city, including Themistocles and Pericles himself, outside the pale of citizenship.

The great idea of Cleisthenes spread with remarkable rapidity throughout the Hellenic world. It was adopted by most states within the Delian confederacy. In the years following 471 B.C. it invaded Peloponnesus itself, and movements leading to democratic consolidation broke out in Elis and Arcadia, which Sparta managed with difficulty to suppress.[1] In 460 B.C. Argos definitely adopted a democratic constitution, modelled on that of Athens. In 415 B.C. an echo of the idea is heard in far-off Syracuse, where Athenagoras, the popular leader, addressing the people, said (Thuc. vi. 39), 'I maintain first and foremost that democracy, in the proper sense of the word, means the whole, while oligarchy designates merely a section or part. Oligarchy does not hesitate to make the masses share its dangers, but when it comes to advantages, it not merely seeks to appropriate these to itself, but holds them as a complete monopoly. On the other hand democracy, while recognizing that the rich are the best guardians of wealth, and the wise the best councillors, insists that the masses can best judge of measures proposed. All these elements, separately and collectively, find their proper level (ἰσομοιρεῖν) in the democratic state.' Thus fifth-century democracy offered for the first time in history an ideal of common justice to mankind, as Alcibiades recognizes when he says 'democracy is the name applied to all that element which stands in opposition to the domination of a privileged class.'[2] The differences between Themistocles and Aristeides, or between Pericles and Thucydides, were no less political than were the issues which divided Pitt and Fox, or Disraeli and Gladstone.

By the close of the fifth century, therefore, Greek political experience, recognizing the potential stasis which lurks in all political association, had arrived at two alternative and contrasting solutions of the problem of government—that of

---

[1] Arist. *Pol.* 1306ᵃ. 12 and 1318ᵇ. 6; Thuc. v. 47. 9; and generally Hill, *Sources*, ch. vii.

[2] vi. 89. 4 πᾶν δὲ τὸ ἐναντιούμενον τῷ δυναστεύοντι δῆμος ὠνόμασται.

oligarchy, the head and centre of which was at Sparta, and that of democracy, which radiated from its source at Athens.

The oligarchical solution, typified by Sparta and maintained by her among her allies in principle, but with much less rigour than that manifested in the leading state itself,[1] was based on the frank recognition that there could be no truly organic relations with the excluded classes. In her institutions Sparta registered her conviction that this was the case, by the brutal declaration of war pronounced annually against the Helots, and by the virtually impassable barriers which she set up against the admission of outsiders to the charmed circle of the peers. Within that circle, quite in the spirit of the American revolutionary who advised his countrymen to hang together, lest they should hang separately, she grossly exaggerated the principle of unity, at the same time confusing the genuinely political bond with what were, strictly speaking, family and economic ties. To crown and reinforce the system, the state arrogated to itself a power of regimentation over the lives of its subjects as terrible in its scope and character as it was appalling in its consequences. Prolonged education, entirely disciplinary in character, taught the rising generation not to turn their faces to the light but to be satisfied to live in darkness, so that in Sparta at least it might be truly said that education was an abortion performed on the mind of the child. If education, however, failed to do its work, the authority of law was invoked to compel obedience, not to the spirit (for that was impossible) but to the letter of Lycurgan institutions. The result was that Sparta and those states which sought to ape her peculiar institutions were really anomalies in fifth-century Hellas. Thus by another path we arrive at the same conclusion as was reached in discussing the external relations of Lacedaemon: 'your institutions are obsolete.'

Yet this is the community which Plato selects as the earthly model for his ethical and metaphysical theory of the state; and,

---

[1] Chios alone, though a member of the Athenian empire, approximated to the social and economic institutions of Sparta. Thuc. viii. 40. 2 οἱ γὰρ οἰκέται τοῖς Χίοις πολλοὶ ὄντες καὶ μιᾷ γε πόλει πλὴν Λακεδαιμονίων πλεῖστοι γενόμενοι καὶ ἅμα διὰ τὸ πλῆθος χαλεπωτέρως ἐν ταῖς ἀδικίαις κολαζόμενοι. viii. 24. 4 Χῖοι γὰρ μόνοι μετὰ Λακεδαιμονίους ὧν ἐγὼ ᾐσθόμην ηὐδαιμόνησάν τε ἅμα καὶ ἐσωφρόνησαν.

in the *Laws*, no less than in the *Republic*, he illustrates the spirit of Spartan institutions rather than those of the genuine City of God. Thus (*Laws*, 716 foll.), after summing up the whole duty of man toward God and his neighbour, he proceeds to claim for the state the right of enforcing this duty. Nothing is excluded from the prerogative which he assigns to the Leviathan. Thought and belief, no less than speech and action, come within its purview and under its control; so that religious and artistic expression, as well as economic and social life, are made the creatures of state authority, and regulated in agreement with the objects which the state has in view. Thus (909 a) we have the Holy Inquisition, armed with power to suppress all forms of nonconformity (909 d), as well as impiety (910 c) either public or private, the extreme penalty for which in all cases is that of death. For moral reasons (915) contracts are restricted to purchase and sale for cash, and all forms of credit are strictly forbidden. Property (913) and the right of testamentary bequest (922) are, in the interest of the family allotments, placed at the mercy of the state and, in the same spirit, the responsibilities and duties of guardians are minutely prescribed (926). The most intimate marital and family disputes (928 d foll.) are settled by public authority. These are but examples, cited at random, to illustrate the truth that, in the Platonic scheme, nothing remains 'private', but every department of life is subjected to the most rigorous control by public authority, and especially by the authority of that sinister institution which Plato appropriately designates the *Nocturnal Council* (960), and which he characterizes as the mind of the state. It is, however, impossible to pass on without allusion to what is perhaps the most amazing feature of government by this ancient prototype of the Ku-Klux-Klan, and that is the number of offences for which it is deemed proper to impose the penalty of death. In one passage indeed (862 d, e) the end of punishment is described as, where possible, remedial, and, where no cure is possible, deterrent and exemplary. Actually, punishment is made to serve throughout as a sort of purge, and the capital penalty is invoked to a degree that is nothing short of incredible, especially in view of the fact that the *Laws*, unlike the *Republic*, embodies Plato's suggestions for a commonwealth which he regards as not merely practicable, but necessary for the salvation of society. Nor is this accidental. It is in fact bound up with the Platonic view of the problem of government; and the same terrorism lurks beneath the surface whenever men endeavour to construct a theory of the state along Platonic lines.

Plato was convinced that the ties of interest were in themselves inadequate to hold society together, without the support of moral and spiritual forces much more potent and deepseated than the most powerful interests can possibly be. And it may be admitted that in his day, as perhaps in our own, speculation tended to exaggerate the rôle which cash-nexus (the bond of common interest) plays in sustaining the vast and complicated fabric of social life. Even for those, however, who agree with Plato in emphasizing the significance of moral and spiritual considerations, this fact by no means justifies the conclusion that the cultivation of moral and spiritual values should be made a prerogative of the state, or in other words that law should be made coextensive with morality, thus confusing the nature and function of both. To do this is to attempt the impossible task of realizing the kingdom of God with the weapons of Caesar. Yet this is precisely what Plato undertakes to do; and he says to all recalcitrants, in the spirit of Robespierre: 'conform or die!' No wonder that, in his opinion, philosophers must be kings or kings philosophers. What earthly government, it may be asked, is either wise or good enough to be entrusted with such powers; especially if it be remembered that to aim so high and miss the goal is to land in the bog of American fundamentalism?

Nevertheless, this attitude has been characteristic of all those who follow Plato in allowing their conception of the state to be dominated by the philosophic point of view. Even Aristotle, for instance, in that portion of the *Politics* in which he seeks to define the state in relation to its ideal end, makes it differ from an alliance on this very point (1280 ᵃ 10–11), although his strong sense of reality forces him to abandon any such criterion when he comes to discuss the practical problems of government in existing states. So long, indeed, as one adheres to the strictly scientific standpoint, it is impossible to admit any such distinction, and the difference between 'state' and 'alliance' lies merely in the infinitely greater number and variety of interests which are shared by those who have in common occupied a clearly defined territory for an immense number of years, so that for them the process of consolidation is virtually complete. Furthermore, science undertakes to trace the rise of states, in many cases beginning either with conquest or with mere alliance, but issuing in genuine 'state-hood', as the threads are slowly woven together to form the tough fabric of a truly communal life. It is also the duty of science to trace the process by which these threads are frayed and broken, until the state disintegrates and disappears. Hence the difficulty which science has in offering an entirely satisfactory definition of the state, a difficulty perhaps greater in theory than in practice, but nevertheless not too easy even in actual life. Are the British Overseas Dominions in fact independent states, in no respect inferior or subordinate to the Mother Land? Nationalists may, in the light of recent declarations by the Imperial Conference, argue that they are. The law, however, reflects but faintly, if it does not always distort, the true significance of all those intangible elements which go to make up the concept of power.

The Platonic idea of the state was revived at the close of the eighteenth century. During the nineteenth it was offered to the world as an alternative to the democratic liberalism popular at that time, and its advocates exalted it as a model by which the actual states of their day should be judged, and which they might well aspire to emulate. To some extent the results were salutary, inasmuch as the Platonic conception involved a trenchant criticism of the ideal of a mere police-state, against the barrenness of which Burke in his day protested, although largely in vain. Dicey[1] traces the stages by which Platonism triumphed successively over this ideal, and over the hardly less inadequate philosophy of individualistic utilitarianism, which, as Ritchie admits,[2] had to discover a way out of its own difficulties, before it could offer an acceptable alternative to the plausible arguments of Plato. As a matter of fact,

[1] *Law and Opinion.*   [2] *Natural Rights*, p. 101.

Ritchie's 'Copernican revolution', by which utilitarianism emancipated itself from its individualistic and hedonistic pre-possessions, came too late to prevent the revived Platonism from firing the public imagination and colouring to a large extent popular views regarding the nature and function of law. 'With every step in the socialization of morals and the moralization of politics something of Greek excellence is won back.' Whoever first uttered this sentiment reflected the enthusiasm of those who longed for a weapon wherewith to smite the Philistines, and found it in the message of Plato. So the Greek came once more into his own, both for good and evil. Modern military conscription is his idea, and so also is modern state education. The state control of economic and social life is also his, and, if his unconscious apostles, especially in the United States of America, wish to discover more forms of prohibition than they have yet been able to invent, they may be confidently recom-mended to search the pages of the *Republic* and the *Laws*, where they may also discover more 'adequate' methods of law-enforcement than they have hitherto devised.

Of recent years, political speculation has reacted against the prescriptions of Plato, and has sought with great earnestness for a definition of liberty more intelligible than that of Rousseau. So violent indeed has been the reaction that in many cases modern doctrine verges on anarchy, and thus the pendulum swings from a blind worship of the state to an equally blind distrust of its power. Because of the excesses of idealism, men take refuge in the excesses of materialism; conscientious objec-tors without consciences are everywhere to be found; and in America active lawlessness[1] is openly recommended as the only possible corrective to the illegitimate extension of law. Through-out the controversy the enemies of Platonism, no less than its friends, have usually assumed that it is representative of the best political thought of Greece.

In so doing they have overlooked the claim of Greek science to be heard as against the pretensions of Greek philosophy. Greek science, whatever may be thought of its beginnings, had by the middle of the fifth century consciously adopted a

[1] As e.g. in the nullification movements.

thoroughly humanistic point of view. This was eminently the case with Protagoras, when he uttered the famous and provocative sentiment: 'Man is the measure of all things.' So far as may be judged from surviving references, it seems to have been not less true in the case of Democritus. The thoroughgoing humanism of fifth-century medicine has already been noted and referred to its background in atomistic thought; it was indeed the first-fruit of the Democritean method. Finally, in the field of politics, science spoke through the mouth of Thucydides, son of Olorus, although the modesty of the guise which he assumed as a mere 'historian' has prevented this truth from receiving the recognition which its importance deserves. For it was in opposition to the ethical and metaphysical points of view that Thucydides described the progress and analysed the issues of the Peloponnesian war.

Thus, for example, with regard to the distinction between oligarchy and democracy, and to the claims which each of these made on the allegiance of men, which was the great political issue of the fifth century B.C., philosophy, seeking to penetrate to the essence of the state, endeavoured to justify the domination of the few over the many, and found such justification in the theory that, while the many were compounded of baser metal, the chosen few were men of gold. Science, on the other hand, was ignorant of any such mysterious distinction in our common clay, and reluctant to apply a criterion so completely beyond the world of sense. Accordingly, science visualized the relations of men as determined by considerations of power and interest. While, therefore, it saw in oligarchy merely the power and interest of a section, it was prepared to recognize the claim of moderate democracy to represent the power and interest of the whole. At the same time it admitted that democracy itself might easily degenerate into sectionalism. Given free rein, the masses no less than the classes might pursue their strictly personal and selfish aims to the detriment of general welfare; and, when that occurred, the results were infinitely more serious even than in the case of oligarchic ascendancy. For oligarchies never claimed to represent anything but the domination of a class, while ochlocracy prostituted to its own base purposes the fair name of government in the interest of the whole.

It is in the light of these considerations that science examined the claims of Periclean Athens, and found on analysis that they represented a reconciliation of interests within the whole, and also the realization of common interests on a scale and to a degree hitherto undreamed of in the political experience of Greece. The same considerations made it possible to lay down the conditions necessary to preserve the state of equilibrium attained in Athens—wisdom, strength, and incorruptibility on the part of the leaders, self-restraint and a disposition to follow sound counsel on the part of those who were led (ii. 65). After the death of the great demagogue, all these principles were thrown overboard (§ 8). The leaders pursued imperial administration in the spirit of adventurers, allowing their personal ambitions and interests to overcome the dictates of sound policy, both at home and throughout the empire. The reason was that they lacked the prestige and judgement of Pericles, who had governed his fellow citizens firmly indeed, but yet in a spirit becoming free men. Lacking his Olympian dignity and power, subsequent leaders embarked on a competition in which they sought to outbid one another for the favour of the masses, and the masses, being deficient in character and self-restraint, accepted their seductive flatteries at their face value. Thus the state, deprived of the guidance of Pericles, slowly disintegrated and collapsed. Yet the resiliency and life of the democratic principle was exhibited even in the hour of Athens' agony (§ 12). She recovered from the Sicilian disaster, and in the end was beaten rather by Persian gold than by the efforts of Sparta; or it would be still more accurate to say that she herself was the cause of her own fall. For the *entente cordiale* between classes having been dissolved, the ugly figure of stasis raised her head, and it was only after Athens had been torn by internal dissension that she surrendered to her enemies and acknowledged complete defeat.

But in 431 B.C. Pericles was still at the helm, and the tragic consequences which the war was to bring upon Athens were as yet unrealized. The question arises: what is to be thought of the claim made on behalf of Periclean democracy and of Greek democracy generally, that it represented the whole people, as opposed to the mere sectionalism of oligarchy, and that its superiority as a principle of government resided in this very fact? In modern times the justice of this claim has been hotly disputed. Attention has been called, not merely to the exclusion of women from all forms of public activity, but to the fact that Greek democracy, no less than Greek oligarchy, was rooted in the black soil of slavery. Mainly on these grounds both forms are lumped together, and dismissed as merely 'dynastic' as compared with the genuine democracy of the modern state.

On the mere level of fact, however, considerable evidence may be found to support the contention that Greek democracy was inclusive in principle, although it may have fallen short of its own standards at various points. Firstly, with regard to the citizen body itself, it must be admitted that, at least from the conclusion of the Persian wars until after the death of Pericles, the substantial middle class of landed proprietors accepted the Cleisthenic form of government, and participated actively in public duties, both military and civil, alongside the commercial class and the proletariat. Of the aristocrats as a group, it can hardly be said that they were ever reconciled to the democratic idea, although individuals may at times have sought to make their way into public life, as Plato himself perhaps did under the restored democracy (*Ep.* 324 C, D). For them, the democratic idea meant that they were deprived of the monopoly of government which their ancestors had enjoyed, and that they could participate in public life only on condition that they submitted to the indignity of suing for popular approval. As most of them were unwilling to do this, they either abstained entirely from politics or, like Antiphon (Thuc. viii. 68. 1), confined their activity to the preparation of briefs for those accused before the popular courts. Yet they continued to live in Athens, enjoying the amenities of social intercourse with one another and with the intellectual lights who, under the patronage of Pericles, frequented the city (Plato, *Dialogues, passim*). The democracy was lenient even to its enemies (Arist. *Ath. Pol.* 22), and could still afford to laugh at the irreconcilable few, who indulged the sense of their own superiority at the price of isolating themselves from the life of the imperial city, leaving it to others to compete for the distinctions which were open to all (Thuc. ii. 37. 1).

In the concluding sentences of the *Funeral Speech* (ii. 45. 2), the speaker briefly dismisses the claims of Athenian women to be anything more than wives and mothers, reminding them that they attain their greatest glory when they measure up to the standards set for them by their own constitution, and their highest reputation when they avoid making themselves the subjects of notice in masculine circles, either for good or evil. In this passage the weight of the argument depends on the phrase 'standards set for them by their own constitution'. Modern society offers innumerable opportunities to women outside the home, in industrial and commercial as well as educational and artistic life; and women have been drawn from domestic seclusion as they have demonstrated their superior (and in some cases unique) qualifications to meet the urgent demands for their services which modern conditions create. In ancient Athens such conditions did not exist. Apart from industry, which was still largely domestic, if it did not involve manual labour too heavy for women's strength, the one great opportunity for employment lay in the public services, civil and military. From such employment women were excluded because of the relative inferiority of their constitution. No abstract question of feminism or anti-feminism comes here into consideration; it is simply affirmed as a fact that women counted for little in the atmosphere of imperial Athens. If, therefore, their position was insignificant, it corresponded with the limited service which they were able to render to society.

The question of slavery in Greece involves the greatest difficulties because of the lack of anything like adequate evidence regarding the numbers of the slaves and the conditions of their employment. It is therefore the duty of students to guard against dogmatizing on the subject. With regard to Sparta, this at least is clear, that the number of helots must have stood to that of the Spartiates as at least seven to one because, when the army took the field, 35,000 helots, armed as light troops,

accompanied the 5,000 Spartan hoplites.[1] Furthermore, it is
no secret that the relations of the Spartans to the helots were
based mainly, if not altogether, upon force, seeing that Lycurgan
institutions were designed to secure the ascendancy of the few
over the many. But the question arises: were not such institutions unique in Greece; and is it not possible that even in the
case of oligarchies which aped Sparta, no such thoroughgoing
system of domination was ever realized? The very ascendancy
of Sparta in Greece depended upon the fact that her allies
relied on her support against revolutionary movements from
within their borders; and, as for the democracies, which had
repudiated such support, they could not have experienced any
great fear of an eruption, at any rate from below.

With regard to Athens, it is generally recognized that there
was a considerable number of barbarian slaves, employed in
the mining operation at Laureion, who must have lived and
worked under conditions that were appalling.[2] Yet, in spite
of this fact, the spirit and atmosphere of the state was that of
liberty and equality. Plato remarks that even the donkeys on
the streets brayed boldly in such an atmosphere. Old Oligarch
(*Ath. Pol.* 10) notes that neither in dress nor appearance was
there any noticeable distinction between slaves, metics, and
citizens. It has been supposed[3] that in industry slave and free-
man worked side by side as mechanics and craftsmen; and this
is certainly the impression which one gets from reading the
passage in Plutarch's life of Pericles, in which he describes
the immense industrial activity in Athens during the brief
period of peace between 440 and 431 B.C., when the temples and
public buildings were restored (Plut. *Pericles,* 12). The truth
seems to be that democratic institutions in Athens were conceived with the idea of securing, as Aristotle says (*Ath. Pol.* 24),
an ample maintenance for a large proletariat, and that they
effected this purpose by an elaborate system of state employment, in time of peace through provision of work in the civil
services or in state-directed industry, in time of war through

---

[1] Hdt. ix. 28. 2, at Plataea. Other references imply that the same proportions were normally observed.

[2] Xen. *Revenues.*   [3] Zimmern, *Greek Commonwealth.*

military and naval employment, for which liberal payment was made.

From the standpoint of numbers, few of the poverty-stricken states of Greece could have possessed sufficient slaves to constitute an important element in the population. Even in imperial Athens the desertion of 20,000 slaves, mostly mechanics, after the Spartan fortification of Decelea, was enough to disrupt the economy of the state (Thuc. vii. 27. 5). Over against these are to be set the numbers of free men, citizens and metics, as they are revealed in the authorities. Thucydides, in his summary of Athenian resources at the beginning of the war (ii. 13), leaves little doubt on this score. The total of those on the catalogue, available for service as knights or heavy armed infantry, amounted to 33,800. Apart from these, Athens put on the sea a fleet of 100 triremes, which, the complement of each ship standing at 200, would make an additional 20,000. These were nearly all thetes, and their number corresponds generally to that given by Plutarch (*Pericles*, 37) when he says that there were exactly 14,040 persons whose right to a share in the corn distribution was admitted and about 5,000 whose claims were rejected because they could not establish their position as citizens. Aristotle also (*Ath. Pol.* 24) notes that during the democratic ascendancy there were approximately 20,000 individuals who got their living from one form or another of public service. The number of metics residing in Athens is unknown, but of these at least 3,000 were qualified by wealth to serve as hoplites, and it has been estimated that their total would fall not far short of 15,000. If this figure were accepted it would give a grand total of free men residing in Attica just short of 69,000, in addition to all those above or below the age for military service. That the figure was at least 50,000 is shown by a reference in Thucydides (iii. 17) in which he states that the largest number of ships put in commission by Athens at one time amounted to 250 (50,000 men), and on this occasion all but the knights, pentacosiomedimni, and metics took a hand at the oar. Every seaman drew the same pay, amounting to one drachma for each day's service. These figures serve in a remarkable way to confirm the repeated statements of our authorities that Athenian democracy was mainly designed to serve the interests of the free poor.

Yet, in the last analysis, the claim that Athenian democracy represented the whole, as opposed to the part, will never be settled on grounds of mere fact; but controversy will rage about the question until agreement is reached regarding the proper method of estimating the justice of the claim. From the standpoint of science, there can be little doubt that Thucydides was right in admitting the contention. Science takes into account merely considerations of power and interest, and from this point of view it can hardly be denied that Athenian democracy conceded to each element within the community the place which its contribution to general stability and well-being enabled it to claim. In spirit the state aimed to be inclusive rather than exclusive. A very liberal franchise gave to individuals and groups a constitutional means of voicing their opinions. Public officials were created, either by lot or ballot, from the citizen body in general, practically without restriction of wealth or birth; and these officials were amenable to the jurisdiction of the popular courts, under such conditions that maladministration involved them in very serious consequences. While the responsibility for public policy rested with the magistrates, and especially with the generals to whom imperial administration was entrusted, there were no constitutional barriers to criticism on the part of private individuals, and these indeed exercised their privilege so freely that magistrates were frequently charged with the execution of policies which they had not initiated, and of which they did not approve. On the other hand, magistrates regularly submitted to the necessity of persuading the assembly to endorse their proposals, so that government really depended on popular opinion, to a degree inconceivable not merely among contemporary oligarchies but even among the parliamentary states of modern times. Thus, as compared with Sparta or any of the other oligarchies, the element of authority and repression was in Athens reduced to a minimum.

In view of this the question may be asked: are not those who brand Athenian democracy as dynastic prompted to do so by a consideration which, whatever may be thought of it, is not strictly scientific? In other words, is not this criticism inspired by the theory of 'natural' rights, which admittedly had no place in the Athenian conception of democracy, but can be traced to its source in Stoic and Christian idealism? In other words, this theory belongs to the world of religion and philosophy rather than to the world of science.

If it is correct to assume that science visualizes the problem of government as the reconciliation of divergent interests and as the realization of common interests within a territorial whole, certain conclusions emerge regarding the nature and purpose of the state. Scientifically, the Cleisthenic idea represented not, as Plato supposes (*Laws*, 700), a declension from the ideal, but rather an advance upon all existing types, inasmuch as it aimed to include all considerable interests within the body politic, and also because, within this wider community, it provided a method for settling controversial issues other than that of force and violence. Thus Cleisthenic democracy offered, if not a cure, at any rate an alternative for stasis, and acceptance of the Cleisthenic principle enabled Athens to staunch, so to speak, the internal wound from which Sparta and the other oligarchies continued to bleed. While, therefore, her rival stood still or actually went back in the course of the fifth century, Athens increased in population and wealth to such a degree that she became a veritable prodigy in the Hellenic world. At the battle of Plataea, Lacedaemon put in the field a force of 10,000 hoplites and 35,000 light armed troops (ix. 10 and 28. 2). Sixty years later, when she was fighting for her life at Mantinea, she mustered, according to the careful calculations of Thucydides (v. 68–9), a hoplite army of 4,184 men. And, whereas the numbers at Plataea represented simply the normal expeditionary force (two-thirds of the whole), the troops that fought at Mantinea included her total available man power, less a division of 837 men detailed to guard the city itself, and comprising those who were either too young or too old to take their places in the fighting line. On the other hand, 8,000 Athenian hoplites fought at Plataea (ix. 28. 6). At the outbreak of the Peloponnesian war she had available a field force of 13,000 hoplites, apart from reserves which brought her total land army up to nearly 34,000 men, and, whereas at Salamis the whole Athenian people were able to man but 180 ships (36,000 men), her available man power fifty years later amounted at least to 50,000 (Thuc. iii. 17), and probably more. In fact, at the outbreak of the Peloponnesian war, her own resources must have been equal to those of all her enemies combined, quite apart from the men and money which she derived from the subject states. Such were the fruits of the democratic principle in terms of wealth and power.

But in order to achieve this immense progress in numbers and resources, the democracy had been forced to sacrifice that peculiar quality of character cherished by aristocracy and dear to the heart of Plato. Instead of seeking to evaluate interests, as Sparta did, Athens merely recognized them; or rather, if she sought to evaluate them at all, she did so not by any absolute moral standard but simply by the standard of public opinion. Thus the democracy resigned any attempt to impose particular moral and religious principles upon its members, and these, together with aesthetic and cultural values, were left to individual judgement (Plato, *Laws*, 700). Even the heresy trial of Socrates, which took place under the restored democracy, was held before a panel of the popular supreme court, and the decision in that case reflected not the authority of a tribunal which claimed divine authority, but merely the prejudices and fears of the average citizen.

In other words, a more limited conception of the functions of the state arose to correspond with the new form. Cleisthenes, while he took the territorial principle as the basis of his division of the people for political purposes, nevertheless 'allowed all persons to retain their family and clan religious rites according to ancestral custom' (*Ath. Pol.* 21). In other words, the democracy abandoned any effective control of belief, at the same time as it repudiated the ancient claim of family and clan to control politics. In instituting new tribal cults for the ten constituencies into which he divided Attica, Cleisthenes simply made use of the still vital force of religion as social and political cement. Ephialtes and Pericles, by destroying the Areopagus, eliminated the last vestige of religious control in the old aristocratic sense, and completely secularized political life. In the *Funeral Speech* Pericles indicates clearly enough that what the state demanded of its citizens was correct action rather than sound belief, and the whole field of belief, as opposed to action, is expressly recognized as falling outside the limits of state-control (ii. 37).

In other words, the democracy restricted its concern to those concrete interests which, as St. Augustine puts it, 'ad mortalem vitam pertinent', and thus for it the problem of statesmanship was summed up in terms of the greatest common welfare. From this point of view, anything capable of being visualized as an interest could be made the subject of political discussion, but if so, it had to be judged by the standard of 'expediency'. The morals of the democratic state were therefore never more than utilitarian morals; and Socrates was condemned, not because he was wrong on a speculative or moral issue, but because his teaching was thought to have an unsettling influence upon Athenian youth.

Thucydides was fully aware that, for democracy, expediency is the rule of state, and there are many passages which could be cited to illustrate this fact. Of these, one in particular may be noticed; viz. the passage in which he analyses the problem of crime and punishment (iii. 37–40). This problem of course arose out of a question of imperial administration, but the discussion is pertinent to the question of domestic government as well, and throws much light on democratic conceptions of law.

It has been observed as a remarkable fact that both speakers—Cleon, into whose mouth is put the argument for severity, and Diodotus, who voices the argument for leniency in the treatment of the rebels—discuss the issue simply on grounds of expediency. This fact ceases to be remarkable if it be remembered that from the democratic (and scientific) standpoint, this is the only ground on which the discussion could logically take place. Cleon begins (37) by observing that, because in democracy the element of authority is so completely submerged and the element of consent becomes so prominent, Athenians forget the truth, that force is really at the bottom of their relations with the allies. 'Your empire is a tyranny.' He then alludes to other characteristics of democratic psychology which unfit the masses for government and, after warning his hearers particularly against the danger of yielding to pity or decency (40 οἶκτος and ἐπιείκεια), he concludes with the appeal that they should exact the extreme penalty as an example to others. Diodotus, replying (42–7), accepts the rule of expediency, and argues against Cleon's proposals on that level. The gravest peril to democracy, he declares, lies in the danger of allowing haste and passion to interfere with full and free discussion, necessary if the true interest of the state is to be discovered. 'Granted', he says, 'that the Mytileneans are utterly wrong, I do not on that account recommend you to put them to death, unless this can be shown to be expedient' (44. 2). 'We are not here to sit in judgement on the justice of the case, but the object of our discussion is to determine what will be most useful' (§ 4). He then (45) launches into a general history of crime and punishment. 'Experience shows that no fear of punishment has been effectual in stopping crime, and it has been found that even the death penalty is no real deterrent. Human nature being what it is, legal prohibitions have never constituted an absolute barrier against wrong-doing. Therefore the law, in framing penalties, has descended to considerations of expediency.' In the present case, the moral is that Athens should refrain from terrifying the masses throughout the empire who are her friends, but who, if the proposals of Cleon are carried out, will be driven to conspire with the oligarchs who are her enemies. These arguments proved effective, and Athens reversed her previous decision to execute the men of Mytilene and to sell the women and children as slaves. Thus, in at least one instance, the cool and dispassionate consideration of what was expedient prevented a horrible crime.

With regard to the problem of government, our analysis has revealed two types of thought and two methods of approach—the one physical and scientific, the other metaphysical and philosophic. The latter, the way of Plato, starts with a vision of what man should be, and seeks to mould actuality to conform

force, for it would prevent him from taking what advantage he can' (i. 76. 2). The same sentiment reappears in the arguments of the Athenians at Melos. 'You know as well as we do that justice according to human standards is determined by the power to enforce it (ἀπὸ τῆς ἴσης ἀνάγκης κρίνεται),' or, in other words, 'justice comes into play only as between equals'. The superior does what he has power to do, and the weak perforce submit (v. 89). 'It is supposed that God and it is known that men always dominate where they can by natural necessity. We did not make this law, nor have we been the first to put it into practice. We have simply taken it over as it existed, and we shall leave it behind us as it is destined to exist for ever. We are satisfied that if you or any one else had the power which we have, you would act in the same way. Naturally, then, seeing that God is power, we have no fear of suffering anything at his hands' (v. 105).

In these passages there is stated in the baldest possible fashion the theory that might is right. In vain the Melians appealed to the common good, the more general expediency (v. 90). In a combat with Athens the chances were overwhelmingly against them, and the imperial city, in the moment of her pride and strength, laughed at the notion that she herself might some day be forced to play the rôle of suppliant (90–103). Vain likewise was the reliance which the Melians placed on the justice of their cause, and on the hope that God and the Lacedaemonians would rise in defence of the right. God, the Athenians argue, will not, and the Lacedaemonians could not, even if they desired to do so, which is not the case, because for them, as for the Athenians themselves, expediency is the rule of life. For the same reason, great powers fear each other less. The appeal of the Melians, whether to expediency or to justice, was pathetically ineffectual. Upon receipt of their ultimatum the Athenians reduced the town, putting to death all who were of military age, and making slaves of the women and children. They then colonized the island, sending thither five hundred settlers of their own.

With regard to the contention that might is right, it is not legitimate to assume that Thucydides accepted the validity of

the Athenian position any more than that, when he described
the subsequent sufferings of the Melians, he meant to imply
that he regarded their fate as just. In the long run, indeed, it
was the Melian position rather than that of the Athenians which
was finally vindicated by events. All that Athenian policy was
able to achieve at Melos was to make a desert and call it peace;
for, if the Melians on their side failed to maintain their independence, the Athenians also failed to assert against them the
authority which they had claimed. To Thucydides, therefore,
the Athenian argument must have appeared to embody the
most dangerous of fallacies, a half-truth; because, while it
expressed correctly enough the formal character of law, namely,
that to exist in any real sense law must be enforceable, it nevertheless ignored the equally important consideration that the
mere possibility of enforcement does not exhaust, or even
touch, the real significance of law. Granted, as the demagogues
maintained, that the Athenian empire was a tyranny, even
tyrants were obliged to go a long way in meeting the wishes of
their subjects, and this indeed was the one condition by which
they might hope to retain their own power (i. 17; vi. 54). In
the evolution of the city states, Athens above all others had
recognized the psychological value of consent, to such a degree
that Cleisthenes had made government by consent the foundation stone of his new constitution; and the reign of law which
ensued in Athens was reflected to some extent in the attitude
which the imperial city adopted toward her allies and depen-
dencies. 'Our subjects', the Athenians declared, 'have become
accustomed to deal with us on equal terms'(i.77.3). 'We deserve
some credit for having refrained from pressing the doctrine
of human inequality to its logical limits, and for acting toward
them in a fashion more equitable than our actual power war-
rants.'[1] The empire, therefore, in its best days had implied a
real reconciliation of interests between rulers and ruled, while
the predominant position which Athens occupied in the confederacy was merely the reflection of her predominant power
to promote the welfare of the whole (i. 75). In other words, the

[1] i. 76. 3 ἐπαινεῖσθαί τε ἄξιοι οἵτινες χρησάμενοι τῇ ἀνθρωπείᾳ φύσει ὥστε ἑτέρων
ἄρχειν, δικαιότεροι ἢ κατὰ τὴν ὑπάρχουσαν δύναμιν γένωνται.

real correlative of power was service, and the truth of this was seen in the fact that throughout the struggle the democracies long continued to support Athenian sway.[1] To this point of view belongs also the argument of Diodotus, in the discussion regarding the punishment to be meted out to the Mytilenean rebels (iii. 46–7). Select your victims, he argues, and make sure of reconciling those whom you cannot suppress. Otherwise the empire will be faced with opposition elements so powerful as to be overwhelming, and will inevitably break down. Thrasymachus, then, overlooks the importance of consent in fixing the new relationships among men. To science, which knows no absolute standards, 'consent' is the equivalent of philosophic 'justice'. Thus there is nothing inherently wrong with empire. On the contrary it expresses a normal relationship among men; but it, like all other forms of government, is justified by its fruits, and their real test is that they succeed in maintaining the active support or at least acquiescence of those subjected to their power.

The same general principles underlay the growth of foreign relations which, like those within the individual commonwealths, depended upon the perception of common interests. Of these interests, not the least vital was that which all parties had in the harmony of Hellenism as a whole, although, unhappily, this interest was but dimly and unequally apprehended in the atmosphere of rivalry which surrounded the city states. Among the additions to the common law during the fifth century, there was none therefore of greater significance than the Peace of 445 B.C., inasmuch as this peace aimed to remove long-standing sources of grievance and to establish conditions making for Hellenic unity. As has already been noted, that instrument substituted for the system of legally autonomous city states an entirely new conception of international (or rather inter-state) relations, as a result of which the Hellenic world was recognized as falling into two great leagues or alliances, within each of which the leading state was to exercise disciplinary powers over the confederates; the treaty providing,

[1] See viii. 73. 6. Samos and the part she played during the oligarchic revolution of 411 B.C.

at the same time, that unenlisted states might join whichever league they preferred. Furthermore, it appears that Athens, at least, agreed that her own port and the ports of her empire should at all times be open to the shipping of Peloponnesus, thus abandoning the right to exert economic pressure upon her rivals by means of embargoes, which were thenceforth recognized as contrary to international law. This at least was the claim advanced by the people of Megara in their recital of grievances against Athens in 431 B.C., although Athens herself seems to have disputed their right of access to her harbour under all circumstances (i. 67. 4 and i. 144. 2). At any rate, she affirmed, this right must be reciprocal if it was not to be meaningless, and the existing restrictions against entrance to Lacedaemon constituted a standing violation of the rule. Finally, the great principle was established that signatories to the treaty should in future submit to compulsory arbitration of all disputes arising between them (vii. 18. 2).

In 433 B.C., therefore, the problem of statesmanship was to estimate the value of the interests to be preserved and of those to be sacrificed by either side. Accordingly, the argument by which the Corinthians sought to prevent the Athenians from making an alliance with Corcyra, takes the form of a statement of claims under international law, especially that portion of it embodied in the treaty.[1] To the best of her ability, she endeavoured to make the Athenians realize that their true interest as an imperial power lay in rejecting the proffered Corcyrean alliance, thus allowing her a free hand in developing her own imperial policy in the north-west. 'If you accept an alliance with these outlaws, you will witness revolts among your own subjects in favour of us, and you will establish the principle to your own detriment rather than to ours' (i. 40. 6). 'The self-sufficiency and independence of their city enables them to set up as judges of their own misdeeds, so that they do not come under the operation of international law. . . . Their isolation (τὸ ἄσπονδον) is a specious pretence which they have thrown up, not in order that they may avoid being dragged into the

[1] i. 41. 1 δικαιώματα μὲν οὖν τάδε πρὸς ὑμᾶς ἔχομεν ἱκανὰ κατὰ τοὺς Ἑλλήνων νόμους.

crimes of others, but in order that they may be free to commit crimes by themselves, and that they may take advantage of their power to act with violence, stealing a point where they can, and avoiding the shame of having their fraud exposed' (i. 37. 3 and 4). These arguments assume that Athens was interested in the maintenance and development of the common law and that, if she could be made to understand the true motives of Corcyrean isolation, she would refuse to link herself in an alliance with Corcyra. Athens, however, preferred the Corcyrean claim that she was a legally independent power and not a rebellious Corinthian colony, or rather, leaving the status of Corcyra an open question, she made a defensive alliance, and was prepared to submit her right to do so to arbitration according to the provisions of the treaty, conscious of the great advantages to be derived from friendly relations with Corcyra, and setting them ahead of any possible danger from Corinthian hostility.

The events which followed demonstrated the ineffectiveness of the great effort of the fifth century to moralize international relations along scientific and utilitarian lines. Corinth, feeling her personal interests touched at a vital point, abandoned all hope of salvation through the treaty. In vain the Athenians drew attention to the incalculable factor in war, urging the Corinthians to consider how great it was before they staked all on the arbitrament of force. 'When war is protracted', they said, 'it usually depends on chances over which both sides equally have no control, and the ultimate outcome is risky and uncertain' (i. 78; cf. i. 122. 1). Their warnings fell on deaf ears. Fear of the old bogey of Athenian expansion blinded the Corinthians to the danger of defeat and disaster, and inspired in them the vain hope that when the Peloponnesians had taught Athens not to meddle in Corinthian affairs, they could bring the war to an end in due course and at the proper moment.[1] Sparta, which, as has already been suggested,[2] had never wholeheartedly accepted the principles of the treaty, disregarded the warnings of her sage and moderate old king, Archidamus,[3]

---

[1] i. 121. 1 ἐν καιρῷ.　　　　　　　　　　[2] Ch. v, above.
[3] i. 79. 2 Ἀρχίδαμος ὁ βασιλεὺς αὐτῶν, ἀνὴρ καὶ ξυνετὸς δοκῶν εἶναι καὶ σώφρων. i. 80. 1 πολέμων ἔμπειρός εἰμι.

whom long experience had taught to measure correctly the unique power and strength of Athens, and the great limitations of Peloponnesian resources and strategy in a contest with the empire. The Spartans repudiated also his advice that they should not declare war, but content themselves for the moment with a protest against the conduct of Athens, while at the same time they embarked on a policy of preparedness and watchful waiting (i. 80–5). Accordingly, under the influence of the Chauvinist ephor Sthenelaidos, the assembly voted that a *casus belli* existed, although with obvious misgivings both as to the justice of their cause and the prospect of victory (i. 87–8). Thus, within fourteen years of the time when it was first adopted, the principle of conciliation was discarded, and force was once more called into play to settle the problems of the Hellenic world.

At the moment when they unsheathed the sword, the Spartans doubtless underestimated the strength of the forces released by their rash act, although they were later to repent the moral offence of which they had been guilty in reintroducing an atmosphere of violence into the public life of Hellas (vii. 18. 2). Pericles, on his part, appears to have felt that in face of the Peloponnesian attitude war could hardly be avoided, and his advice to his fellow citizens was that they should stand firm. The refusal of the Spartans to arbitrate was, he declared, the final link in a long chain of evidence going to prove that they resented the existence of the empire and plotted its destruction. 'They wish to resolve the differences between us by war rather than by discussion, and they now approach us with a series of orders rather than complaints.' To yield to any one of their demands would be to surrender all future liberty of action. The final answer of Athens must be to repeat the offer of arbitration, at the same time affirming her own pacific intentions, but warning the other side that she would defend herself if attacked. His advice was accepted, and a formal declaration by Athens of loyalty to the principles of the treaty was the last note sounded before negotiations were finally suspended, while the Greek world awaited with tense excitement the onrush of the coming storm.

On either side, a cold prognostication of the chances of victory

exposed in all its naked horror the true character of the method
which had now been adopted for the purpose of settling the
differences of Hellenism. War is antagonism, in which the
consciousness of power is all but completely unrestrained by
a sense of responsibility toward opponents, while reason, put
at the service of self-preservation, devotes itself to devising
ways and means for breaking down the resistance of the enemy.
The Peloponnesians, on their part, could hardly hope to compel
a decision by their own unaided efforts in the field. For them,
therefore, the chance of victory depended upon their ability to
stir up revolts among the subjects of the empire; and this, in
turn, meant that they must wrest control of the sea from the
Athenians. But the resources of Corinth, their one source of
financial support, were not to be compared with those of Athens.
The Dorian cities of Magna Graecia were remote, and had
interests of their own to sustain, although something might
be effected among them by appealing to the indefinite Spartan
claim of hegemony (ii. 7. 2), and by raising the race cry of
Dorian against Ionian. The barbarians alone possessed the
resources necessary to enable the Peloponnesians to equip and
maintain a fleet capable of challenging the sway of the mistress
of the seas. Victory, therefore, over the Athenians was to be
purchased only at the price of fomenting stasis throughout the
Hellenic world, and of betraying the cause of Hellenism to the
Persians. That price the Spartans, although with shame and
reluctance, were ultimately compelled to pay (viii. 18, 37, 43, 58).

It has been questioned whether the Peloponnesians, at any
rate in the initial stages of the war, contemplated the introduction of barbarian aid to turn the scale against her enemies, but
the evidence reported by Thucydides is strongly in favour of
the view that they did. Apart from the references to possible
barbarian assistance in the speech of Archidamus (i. 82. 1),
there is the definite statement that the Peloponnesians made
immediate preparations to send an embassy not merely to the
Great King but elsewhere among the barbarians, for the purpose
of invoking aid (ii. 7. 1). In the autumn of 430 B.C. these
deputies were actually intercepted in Thrace by the pro-
Athenian monarch Sitalces, turned over by him to the Athenians,

and by them put to death (ii. 67. 4). At the close of the year 425, Artaphernes, an emissary from the king proceeding to Sparta, was arrested by Athenian troops at Eion on the Strymon, and a document found on his person revealed the fact that the Spartans were in constant communication with the national enemy, although the king found it difficult to interpret their real wishes, because no two of their deputations made the same proposals (iv. 50). Negotiations, delayed for many years by Spartan reluctance to pay the price, finally came to a head in the series of treaties, quoted by Thucydides in his eighth book. In the first of these (viii. 18) a pact was made, by which the Spartans admitted the right of the king to possession of 'all the territory and all the cities possessed by the king himself or by his ancestors'. Strictly speaking, this would have given the king a title to the whole coast of Asia, the Propontis, and the Balkan area as far as the borders of Thessaly, and would thus have thrown away the gains of the century. Such an arrangement was too much even for Spartan pride to swallow, and as a matter of fact, the publication of this document would have exposed the insincerity of Spartan professions, and hardened the resistance of Hellas against her (viii. 43). Consequently, the Spartan command succeeded in bringing about successive modifications of the original treaty, in which the claims of the king were whittled down, so that he was finally recognized merely as the legitimate ruler of Asia. Even this, however, was enough to prove that the Spartans, in their anxiety to destroy the Athenian empire, were willing to betray the liberties of Hellas.

With regard to the prospects of the war, the Athenians were confident of the purely military issue so long as they could maintain command of the sea. There was but one danger which Pericles apprehended. This was that the Athenians should forget the purely defensive objects which they had in view and that, as temptations multiplied and restraints vanished, they should abuse the power which they possessed through command of the sea. This danger, however, was inherent in the very nature of war, and to it the Athenians, because of their temperament, were peculiarly exposed. Perhaps, therefore, because of its very seriousness, Pericles at first alluded to it only in the vaguest of terms (i. 144. 1); and in his efforts to avoid it he based the strategy of Athens on purely defensive principles to correspond with her war aims, with results which were unfortunate both for the morale of the people and for his own prestige (ii. 12. 13, 18–22, 59–65). Then, as the strain tightened, and means had to be taken to raise the spirits of his countrymen, he himself was compelled to reveal to them something of the offensive as well as defensive significance of sea power, thus throwing out the dangerous hint which aroused their predatory instincts and led ultimately to the ruin of the state (ii. 60–4). In this way the scoff which Alcibiades flung at those who opposed his grandiose schemes was shown to be well founded. It proved impossible to control the limits of an empire as though it were a household, especially in time of war. The expansionist forces of Athenian imperialism were released, and with the cry of 'endless employment' on their lips, the Athenians plunged headlong into the most terrible disaster which ever befell an Hellenic state (vi. 18. 3; 24. 3; vii. 87. 5).

The picture of war presented by Thucydides is one of un- relieved and ever deepening gloom. 'In peace and prosperity both states and individuals have better sentiments because they are not swept along by imperious necessity. But war, by taking away the easy provision of daily needs, proves a rough teacher, who generally assimilates the dispositions of men to their cir- cumstances' (iii. 82. 2). Faced with the grim alternative of conquest or destruction, the combatants exhibited a growing tendency to fight with any or every weapon which came to hand. The need of Sparta to acquire a navy and her willingness to accept the assistance of Persia to this end have already been noted. In the meanwhile, to compensate for her maritime inferiority, she embarked on a campaign of 'frightfulness' at sea. Her privateers, taking refuge along the inhospitable coast of Caria and Lycia, issued forth to prey on the trade from Phoenicia to Greece (ii. 69). Here and elsewhere, in their efforts to paralyse the commerce of the empire, the Spartans adopted the policy of systematically destroying as enemies all persons whom they captured at sea, whether they were allies of the Athenians or neutrals (ii. 67. 4). In so doing, they dealt a blow to that confidence upon which the common law of Greece was erected, and provoked, on the part of the Athenians, a retaliation which was equally subversive of the law of nations. For the Athenians, when the Peloponnesian deputies who had been arrested by Sitalces were turned over to them, executed summary justice upon them without formal trial and without giving them the opportunity to make a statement, thinking it proper to defend themselves by the same methods which the Spartans had initiated when they murdered Athenian and allied traders at sea (*l.c.*). At the beginning of the struggle there was widespread apprehension among the enemies of Athens, that she meant to array the barbarian levies of Thrace against her opponents in Greece (ii. 101. 4). This was not at that time the case, although barbarians were freely employed on both sides in the campaigns for control of the north (iv. 103 foll.). Subsequently, however, as additional man-power was needed, Athens engaged and, except for an accident, would have employed, the services of Thracian mercenaries as reinforcements against Sicily (vii. 29. 1). The savage behaviour of these Thracians during their return home vividly revealed the character of the weapons which Greeks were willing to employ in a conflict with Greeks. Wantonly falling upon the little Boeotian town of Mycalessus which, confident of security, lay open to their assault, they sacked the houses and temples and slaughtered the inhabitants, sparing neither young nor old, but cutting down every living thing which they encountered, not excepting the beasts of burden in the streets. They even fell upon a boys' school, into which the children had just entered, and massacred them every one. Appalled by the horror of this crime, so sudden and so terrible, even the reserve of Thucydides breaks down; and he concludes his account by observing that no disaster more lamentable occurred during the whole war (vii. 29–30). Yet, as the struggle wore on, the Greeks themselves exhibited in their treatment of one another conduct which would have disgraced even the barbarians.

The demoralizing results of the appeal to the sword began to manifest themselves even before any formal declaration of war. Throughout the Hellenic world the oligarchical factions, which had never in their hearts accepted the democratic principle of government by consent as an adequate equivalent of aristocratic 'justice', hailed with delight the prospect of a conflict in which they saw an opportunity of recovering their lost ascendancy by force of arms, and they interpreted the pronouncement of Sparta in favour of autonomy as a promise that she would support their efforts to overthrow the local democracies. Accordingly, the oligarchical faction in Plataea immediately conspired to open the gates by night to an armed band of Thebans, willing, as Thucydides observes, for the sake of their personal power, to destroy those of their fellow-citizens who opposed them and to make over the city to the Thebans (iii. 20–4 and 65. 2). Thus the mere prospect of war sufficed to stir up revolutionary movements in Plataea, in the course of which fellow-citizens butchered one another, and the democrats all too soon learned the lesson of violence and fraud from their opponents. Their feuds led ultimately to the expulsion of the oligarchs, and involved the town in a siege by the combined forces of Boeotians and Peloponnesians, which gave Thucydides an opportunity of describing siege operations as they existed at the beginning of the war. The siege, prolonged through the winter of 429/8 by the inefficiency of the attackers and the gallantry of the defence, was finally concluded by the capitulation of the town, although only after almost half of the Plataeans had succeeded in breaking through the lines and making their escape to Athens (iii. 22–4 and 52). The appeal of the surviving remnant for mercy, both on the grounds of their past services to Hellenism and because of their voluntary surrender, was disregarded by the Spartans, who callously conceded to the malevolence of Thebes the destruction of the famous little city and the butchery or enslavement of its inhabitants (iii. 53–9; 61–7, and 68).

The revolt of Mytilene from Athens was an ill-conceived venture, based on the apprehension of future maltreatment at the hands of Athens rather than on any concrete act of injustice which she had already suffered (iii. 9–14), and encouraged by the belief that, the imperial city being incapacitated by the plague, the moment had come when, with Peloponnesian aid, Lesbos might hope to reassert her freedom. Events showed that the revolt had been fomented merely by a narrow oligarchical group; for when, as time went on, the promised assistance failed to arrive, and it became necessary for the government to arm the masses, the latter at once got out of hand, and compelled the Lesbian general to surrender at discretion to the Athenian admiral who was besieging the city. We have already alluded to the debate which subsequently took place at Athens concerning the punishment to be meted out to the prisoners. The case for severity, which Thucydides puts into the mouth of Cleon, drew its real strength from the moral indignation of the Athenians at what they considered to be an act of the blackest treachery and ingratitude, and during the brief period in which the mood lasted, it enjoyed a momentary triumph. But Thucydides, as though anxious to show that, despite the war, some degree of sanity and humane feeling survived in the atmosphere of Athens, records the fact that the assembly by a narrow majority supported the plea of Diodotus, and by an almost superhuman effort succeeded in saving the Mytileneans from their fate. That fate was no different from the fate so callously imposed by the Spartans upon the men of Plataea, and it is a melancholy commentary on the degradation of moral standards brought about by the war that, after ten years more of conflict, the Athenians themselves had so far degenerated as to inflict upon Melos the very treatment which they had shrunk from inflicting upon Mytilene, although in the latter case the provocation was infinitely greater than in the former.

During the whole twenty-seven years of fighting, there arose but one favourable opportunity of bringing the struggle to an end, on terms which would not only have been acceptable to Sparta as well as to Athens, but which would have vindicated the cause for which Pericles had stood at the beginning of the war. That opportunity presented itself as a result of the fortunate accident at Pylos. The Spartans, failing to dislodge the Athenians from the post which they had improvised on the coast of Messenia, and learning with consternation that a considerable section of the relieving troops had been cut off on the island of Sphacteria, promptly lost the will to fight, and sent a deputation to Athens for the purpose of obtaining peace on any tolerable terms (iv. 3–5, 8–20). 'Now if ever', they declared, 'is the time of reconciliation for us both, before anything irremediable occurs between us, as a result of which we must be involved in undying personal hatred over and above the common hostility which divides us. . . . Let us be reconciled while the contest is still undecided, and you may acquire glory and our friendship, while we, averting disgrace, may have means of repairing our disaster on tolerable terms. Let us choose for ourselves peace instead of war, and at the same time relieve the other Greeks from their afflictions' (iv. 20).

The occasion was propitious, and the argument for peace by agreement could not have been more strongly stated. When she entered the war, Athens had done so without either the wish to destroy Sparta, or the means to achieve that end. As for the recovery of her land empire in Greece, that was equally beyond her hopes or powers. The First Peloponnesian war had shown that, burdened as she was by her imperial commitments, she could not aspire to conquest within the peninsula itself; and the issue, so far as Pericles was concerned, had been settled by the terms agreed to in the treaty of 445 B.C. If, then, the war on Athens' side had been undertaken for the purely defensive purpose of vindicating her claim to freedom of action under the treaty, it would appear that this purpose had been achieved when the Spartans presented themselves with an appeal for peace; and it is unlikely that Sparta, disappointed and dispirited by the outcome of the fighting, would soon have challenged the might of Athens on the same issue again.

This was the view taken by moderate men in Athens, and it can hardly be questioned that it met with the endorsement of Thucydides. Apart from the fact that he displays throughout his confidence in Nicias, who at this time put himself at the head of the forces making for peace, and that he does not seek to conceal his hatred and contempt for Cleon, who was the leader of the Die-hards, the project of a peace by agreement must have commended itself to him, in view of the obvious equality of the conflicting forces, and the so far inconclusive results of the struggle. Scientific realism concerns itself with nothing but interests and the power to maintain them; and one of the greatest of all realists subscribes to the position of Thucydides, when, speaking of another occasion in many ways curiously analogous to this, and using words which might easily be an actual translation of those which Thucydides puts into the mouths of the Spartans, he says: 'Hoc unum esse tempus de pace agendi, dum sibi uterque confideret et pares ambo viderentur. Si vero alteri paulum modo tribuisset fortuna, non esse usurum condicionibus pacis eum qui superior videretur, neque fore aequa parte contentum qui se omnia habiturum confideret.'[1]

'Thus spoke the Lacedaemonians, thinking that the Athenians, who had formerly been desirous of making terms with them, and had only been prevented from doing so by their own refusal, would now, when peace was offered to them, joyfully agree' (iv. 21. 1). With these words Thucydides introduces his explanation of how the opportunity for reconciliation was lost, and both parties were committed to a continuation of the struggle, during which the issues became so complicated that the peace made by Nicias, when it did come, proved impossible to enforce. The fomenter of discord was Cleon, the same demagogue who, at an earlier stage of the war, had employed his powers of persuasion to advocate a policy toward the allies which would speedily have disrupted the empire. On this occasion, Cleon encouraged the natural desire of the Athenians to press their advantage, and induced them to raise once more the issue which had been settled against them in 445 B.C., by demanding what virtually amounted to a restoration of their land empire (iv. 21). When the Lacedaemonians, without either openly refusing or acceding to this outrageous request, asked merely for the privilege of discussing terms in private with commissioners to be appointed by the Athenian people, the demagogue assailed them in unmeasured language,[2] accusing them of dishonest intentions, and demanding that they state their proposals before the assembly. 'Open diplomacy', as all

---

[1] Caesar, *Bellum Civile*, iii. 10. 7
[2] iv. 22. 2 Κλέων δὲ ἐνταῦθα δὴ πολὺς ἐνέκειτο.

sensible persons must have recognized, was impossible in such circumstances, and the Lacedaemonian deputation reluctantly abandoned negotiations, their errand having proved fruitless.

Subsequent events offered an example of what to philosophy may appear to be the power of a transcendental Fortune, but what science must regard merely as a happy accident such as all men are conscious of having experienced in the course of their lives; in this sense, that the outcome was unwarranted by any rational calculation of ends and means. The efforts of the Athenians had failed to reduce the Spartiates imprisoned on Sphacteria, for reasons which were in no sense mysterious but the natural consequence of their attempt to invest an island in the face of lack of food and water, a confined space for their camp, the impossibility of anchoring close to shore, and the fact that the Spartans had bribed the Helots with offers of freedom and monetary rewards to convey supplies to the besieged (iv. 26). In these circumstances, the boast of Cleon that, given the opportunity, he himself would reduce the place, was quite ridiculous. Called upon to make good his boast, the wily demagogue had wit enough to summon to his assistance the experienced general Demosthenes. The latter, with the experience of bush warfare which he had acquired in Aetolia, was just the person needed for the task, and it was his skill which in reality brought the affair to a successful conclusion (iv. 30–8).

The overwhelming impression produced in Hellas by such an unprecedented event as the surrender of the Spartiates was capitalized by Cleon, and the prestige which he had acquired was used by him to prevent the acceptance of a second Lacedaemonian offer of peace (iv. 41). Sparta, demoralized by a rapid succession of reverses, would in all probability have collapsed, had it not been for the action of Brasidas (55 foll. and 70). This man, previously noted as the first Spartan to win public distinction in the war (ii. 25), perceived the one vulnerable point in the Athenian empire. Collecting a handful of men, he pushed his way through Thessaly to the Thraceward regions where, by a judicious appeal to the principle of autonomy and by the use which he made of anti-Athenian sentiment in Macedonia, he won a series of rapid successes

which greatly embarrassed the Athenians and served to revive
the morale of Sparta. Thus the balance of conflicting forces,
so nearly overturned, was once more restored. After the death
of Brasidas, the Amphipolitans paid him the honours of a hero
and founder (v. 11), but to science the real significance of his
career lay in the example which he had given of his essentially
human qualities of leadership.[1] In the deaths of Brasidas and
Cleon, Thucydides saw the removal of the two greatest forces
making for a continuation of the war (v. 16). The subsequent
peace, based as it was on a return to the *status quo* (v. 18–20),
reflected the generally indecisive character of the fighting, but
nevertheless marked the failure of Sparta to make good the
claims, to vindicate which she had unsheathed the sword.
However, it came too late. The treaty, though ratified by a
majority vote of the Peloponnesians, was unacceptable not
merely to the Thebans, Eleans, Megarians, and Corinthians,
but also the Chalcidian cities to whose freedom Brasidas had
pledged the faith of Sparta. The unwillingness of some parties
and the inability of others to implement its terms led inevitably
to a renewed outbreak of hostilities. Thus Brasidas and Cleon
had each in his own way done his work, and the one great
opportunity for a reconciliation of Hellas was forever lost.

The Peace of Nicias having failed, it became the duty of the
historian to trace the forces leading to a revival of active
hostilities, and to demonstrate the unity of the war (v. 26); at
the same time carrying the narrative to its conclusion and noting
the circumstances under which Greeks and barbarians were
drawn into the vortex, until the struggle became in fact a world
war. His method throughout remained the same—a model of
scientific humanism, which sought for the causes of phenomena
in observable 'physical shocks'.

In 431 B.C. the Sicilian Greeks were still, as they had been
during the Persian invasions (Hdt. vii. 153–67), removed by distance and sentiment from the main current of Hellenic affairs,
although their general affiliations were with Dorian Peloponnese,
and the Lacedaemonians had ordered them to furnish a fleet

[1] See especially his speech to the troops when threatened with panic,
iv. 126.

(Thuc. ii. 7). Nevertheless, their economic importance was extremely great, and this fact, already noted by Herodotus (*l. c.*), was emphasized by Thucydides, both in his account of the settlements of Magna Graecia (Thuc. vi. 1–6) and elsewhere. It was natural, therefore, that the eyes of both contestants should have been turned to the west at an early stage of the conflict, with a view to making any possible use of the forces contained in Magna Graecia, and at the same time preventing their employment by the enemy. This was the meaning of the first Athenian expedition sent to Sicily under Laches in 427 B.C. 'The Athenians sent the [twenty] ships, nominally because of their affiliations [with the Chalcidian cities], but actually because they did not wish the Peloponnesians to obtain grain from Sicily. Furthermore, they meant to test the possibility of bringing the power of Sicily into their own hands' (iii. 86. 4). Subsequently, when the conflict in continental Greece had ended in stalemate and yet, because of the failure of the Peace of Nicias, the combatants were committed to a renewal of the struggle, Athens was compelled by the logic of sea power to risk the great Sicilian expedition, as the only means of bringing to bear on the Peloponnesians a mobilization of force so powerful as to be overwhelming.

The project, desirable as it was in the circumstances, was rendered the more tempting by anticipation of easy success. Carried away by the arguments of Alcibiades and by their own hopes, the Athenians paid no attention to the gloomy forecasts of Nicias; or rather, accepting his views regarding the magnitude of the task, they voted troops and supplies on such a scale as to commit themselves to the venture almost beyond the possibility of withdrawal. Alcibiades in 416 B.C. advocated the expedition on general grounds of policy. You cannot, he declared, control the limits of empire. The true defensive is a vigorous offensive, and Athens, if she once obtains control of Sicily, will be irresistible in the Greek world (vi. 18). On the other hand, Sicily itself invited attack. Her huge population was no cause for alarm, because of its mixed character, and the fact that there was no local or general patriotism in the island and no regular system of defence. 'They are a motley crew, who are never of

one mind in counsel, and are incapable of any concerted action'
(vi. 17. 4).

That these arguments were not without foundation is confirmed by the analysis of the situation already given by Thucydides in his account of the conference of Gela, held in 424 B.C.,
as a result of the first Athenian expedition to Sicily (iv. 58–64).
In that conference Hermocrates of Syracuse had emphasized one
aspect of the Athenian peril which was frequently overlooked,
namely, that the intervention of the empire was normally
occasioned by local disputes, in the course of which contend-
ing factions sought a make-weight against their enemies in
the support of Athens.[1] 'I do not blame them', he declared, 'for
their desire to rule, so much as those who are willing to submit
to their sway. It is human nature always to assert authority
over those who yield to it' (61. 5). The same general principles
were later stated from the Athenian point of view at the conference of Camarina (vi. 82–8). On them Hermocrates founded
his plea for harmony in Sicily as the only means possible of
keeping the island free from the Athenian menace and the
plague of war. As peace, he argued, is the greatest of all
blessings, let us compromise our claims against one another
and be reconciled (63–4). For the moment his views triumphed,
and the ready acceptance by the delegates of the principle
'Sicily for the Sicilians' led to the immediate evacuation of the
island by the Athenian troops (65).

It was a revival of the stasis deplored in 424 B.C. by Hermocrates that led to the great Athenian expedition nine years later.
The Segestans, desirous of crushing Selinus at any price,
invoked the aid of Athens (vi. 6); and the Athenians, in their
eagerness to get a fresh foothold on the island, allowed themselves to be deceived by stories of their fabulous wealth
(vi. 8 and 46). In Syracuse, Hermocrates was discredited
because of his oligarchical predilections, and his warnings of
danger were completely disregarded by the democracy of that
city (38). Thus circumstances favoured the enterprise; and the
anticipation of victory for Athens was endorsed by Thucydides

[1] iv. 61. 1 χρὴ . . . νομίσαι τε στάσιν μάλιστα φθείρειν τὰς πόλεις καὶ τὴν
Σικελίαν.

himself when he declared that the expedition failed, not because of any miscalculation of the enemy's power, but rather because the popular leaders, instead of consulting for the interests of the expedition which they had sent out, occupied themselves with intrigue for the leadership of the democracy, thus not only hampering the operations of the army, but occasioning, for the first time, broils in the city itself (ii. 65. 11).

A comparison between the Sicilian expedition and the account given by Herodotus of the invasion of Xerxes reveals the immense advance in standards of historical interpretation achieved within a single generation. The motives of the expedition, as recorded by Thucydides, were purely physical (vi. 1, 6, 8–29). Its tragic failure was ascribed by him to causes of the same order. Most important of these perhaps was the party feeling in Athens, to which allusion has just been made; the first-fruit of which was the divided command, while the second was the agitation against Alcibiades which arose from his alleged profanation of the mysteries and culminated in his recall, thus turning him from a friend of Athens into her implacable and deadly foe. A recent writer[1] has noted the difficulty of the project from the purely military point of view. With an army, inferior in numbers to what they expected to meet, supported by a greatly superior fleet, the Athenians set out to conquer Sicily. The army was defeated. To supplement the deficiencies of the army on land the fleet was moved into the harbour, where it gradually deteriorated. Finally, it was forced to fight inside the harbour, where its tactical superiority was sacrificed, since that depended upon superior speed on the open sea. The result was the defeat of the fleet and the total destruction of both fleet and army.'[2] The one chance of victory for the Athenians lay in taking advantage of the unprepared condition of Syracuse, and in making an immediate assault upon the city (vi. 47–50). This plan, proposed by Lamachus, was rejected because of the opposition of Nicias, whose temperamental and physical incapacity for leadership in

[1] Custance, *A Study of War*, p. 9.
[2] *Vide* especially Thuc. vii. 11–15.

such a venture revealed itself throughout the operations, and was so obvious to himself that he begged to be relieved of his command (vii. 15). The faith, however, which the Athenians had in Nicias as a man and a statesman, led them to put unwarranted confidence in him as a soldier, and gave him the power to veto the successive proposals of Demosthenes, which might have saved the armament even in its extremity (vii. 47–72). These reasons among others led to the failure of the expedition, but a last cause remains to be noted, significant in itself and also because it illustrates the faith of Thucydides in the democratic principle. 'In the Sicilian cities alone the Athenians encountered an enemy similar in character to themselves, organized as they were on democratic lines, and strong in ships, cavalry, and population. They were not able to introduce an element of discord among them and gain them over by holding out to them the prospect of a change of government, nor could they overcome them by bringing to bear upon them a marked superiority of force' (vii. 55. 2). Thus the disaster at Syracuse illustrates not so much the power of Fortune as the incapacity of men to prognosticate the outcome of a venture so vast in scope and attended by so many complicating circumstances.

To Thucydides, there was no phenomenon connected with the war more sinister and more malign than that of this discord or *stasis*, the strife which arises within the community, perverting every human instinct, and disrupting and destroying the normal associations of men. To him, as we have seen,[1] civil society represented the triumph of wisdom and power over this principle of disintegration, which nevertheless lay dormant, so to speak, within the bosom of the community, requiring only a sufficient shock to bring it out, with results that were always disastrous, and seldom less than fatal. That shock was provided by the war. 'Through stasis there fell upon the cities many terrible calamities, such as occur and are always destined to occur so long as the nature of men remains the same, varying in intensity and form according to the shock' (iii. 82. 2).

The state, as Thucydides understood it, was an organization

[1] Ch. iv, above.

of power, by means of which its members obtained for themselves security and concrete well-being; and this power was
measured by the degree to which these advantages were extended among the citizens, and the numbers of those who
participated in them. From this point of view democracy was
a stronger form of organization than its rival, oligarchy; for,
although in both types force was to some extent necessarily
present, the element of repression was in oligarchies offset
merely by habit and fear, while the democratic principle of
government by consent afforded a general assurance that the
compulsion of the state would never be applied where it could
not be made effective. Naked force, however, was by itself
insufficient to keep society together. Yet the war, which was
an appeal to force, suggested to men that the true method of
solving not merely their inter-state but also their domestic
problems was that of antagonism; and, in the atmosphere of
violence thus created, this method was everywhere adopted, so
that stasis spread like a contagion throughout the Hellenic
world. Naturally enough, it descended first upon the oligarchies,
in which the roots of communal life had not attained any great
depth; but, as the shock of war was intensified, it attacked the
democracies also, so that it became at last the melancholy duty
of the historian to analyse the disruption of society even in
Athens.

We have already noted the outbreak of revolutionary spirit
in Plataea and in Mytilene. The first great community, however, to suffer complete destruction from stasis was Corcyra
(iii. 70–83; iv. 46–8). In this city the rival factions, supported
alternately by the presence of Peloponnesian or Athenian ships,
profited by the occasion to massacre their opponents, and their
feuds continued until at last the oligarchical party was completely extinguished, and there was not more than a remnant
of the democrats left to take victorious possession of the island.
Subsequent revolutions were each worse than the earlier, both
in the cunning of the plots and the diabolical cruelty of the
counter-plots. Yet, because it was typical, Thucydides pauses
in his account of the Corcyrean stasis, to offer a general analysis
of the revolutionary spirit (iii. 81–3, and possibly 84). This

analysis, which begins with a κατάστασις, and then proceeds to a description of symptoms, curiously resembles that of the plague at Athens, but unlike it concludes with a prognosis or classification in which the phenomena are related to one general cause (iii. 82. 8). No mere paraphrase could possibly approach the brilliance of the analysis, the sum and substance of which is that exaggerated egoism, arising from avarice and ambition, together with the partisan feeling which carries them along, leads to a pathological condition closely approaching insanity. The competitive principle, seeking realization within society by the method of antagonism suggested by the war and by it released from the restraints of moral and social convention, perverts every normal human purpose and instinct upon which society rests, and leads to the collapse of the state.

In the *Funeral Speech* Pericles had boasted that Athens had solved the problem of social strength and well-being, although it is apparent that he himself feared the outbreak of stasis in the city even at the beginning of the war (ii. 12. 2). Nicias, pathetically echoing the words of Pericles in his last address to the troops, exhorted his fellow-citizens to fight for their lives and for the 'freest country in the world, where there is no interference with the daily life of any man' (vii. 69. 2). Even Phrynichus, on the eve of the revolution of 411 B.C., was able to compare oligarchy with democracy, very much to the disadvantage of the former. 'As for the so-called nobility,' he declared, 'they were the persons who suggested crimes to the popular mind; who provided the means for their execution; and who reaped the fruits themselves. As far as it rested with the oligarchy, the punishment of death would be inflicted unscrupulously and without trial, whereas the people brought the oligarchs to their senses, and were a refuge to which the oppressed might always have recourse' (viii. 48. 6). Such was the confidence which Athenians of all political stripes had in their institutions and in the democratic principle.

Nevertheless, the shocks of the war, following one on the other, together with the prolonged hardship and suffering which it entailed, slowly wore down even the resistance of Athens until she was finally engulfed in a cataclysm similar in character to that which destroyed Corcyra. In 431 B.C., Pericles had visualized a war which, on the side of Athens at least, would not be a war; in this sense, that he sought to keep the citizens free from exposure to the shocks involved in conflict. Yet this was shown, even in his lifetime, to be impossible. The removal of the country population into the city disturbed the normal conditions of life for a large section of the population, and created for the government a powerful opposition element which, while it expressed itself as yet through normal political channels, was nevertheless strongly suggestive of potential stasis (ii. 16–22). We have already described the appalling consequences of the plague.[1] Of these, the most serious was the collapse of moral standards, the result of a shock which neither religion nor convention was able to resist.[2] As a consequence, men sought the good in those immediate and selfish gratifications, which alone seemed to survive the general wreckage, and the eloquence of Pericles was only partially successful in recalling them to a sense of the more permanent values to be achieved within the social whole (ii. 60–4). After his death conditions rapidly went from bad to worse. The mutilation of the Hermae and the profanation of the Mysteries took place at a moment when the people were keyed to the highest pitch of excitement by the Sicilian expedition (vi. 27–8 and 60–1). In the manifestation of religious and mob psychology which followed, the city underwent an experience similar to those outbursts of 'religio' to which even the stolid Romans were subject when exposed to the strain of war; and for which the latter had a cure evidently unknown or inapplicable to the more enlightened society of Athens. Thus, unlike the Romans, the Athenians resorted to the expedient of a blood-letting, which, as Thucydides remarks, had a beneficial effect on the city, although no one could say whether or not the sufferers were justly punished (vi. 60. 5). The dark suspicion that the incident portended a conspiracy aiming at tyranny or oligarchy (60–1), together with the savage injustice of the cure, revealed a sharp declension

---

[1] Ch. iii, above.
[2] ii. 53. 3 προσταλαιπωρεῖν τῷ δόξαντι καλῷ οὐδεὶς πρόθυμος ἦν. § 4 θεῶν δὲ φόβος ἢ ἀνθρώπων νόμος οὐδεὶς ἀπεῖργε.

from the atmosphere of confidence and concord, in which alone
a free government is possible. These shocks, however, great
as they were, were insufficient to break down the tough fabric
of communal life. Even after the appalling disaster in Sicily,
the imperial city once more raised her head (viii, *ad init.*) and
prepared to face sufferings, through the fortification of Decelea
and the loss of Euboea, beside which her previous troubles,
great as they were, paled into insignificance (vii. 26–8 and
viii. 96). But at last the slow process of attrition did its work,
and toward the close of his eighth book, Thucydides portrays
the first of those mighty convulsions which rent the city and
portended its final fall.

It would be an exaggeration to assert that in the view of
Thucydides war is insanity. Nevertheless, it remains true that,
according to his doctrine, the fierce antagonisms of conflict tend
to produce conditions in which the human mind is finally
unbalanced. Speaking of the epidemic at Athens, Thucydides
had observed that those who, while still immune from the
disease, attempted to help the sufferers, themselves as a rule
fell victims, paying for their unselfish idealism with their lives
(ii. 51. 5). The war as a whole gave rise to shocks analogous to
but more severe even than the shock of the plague; so that, as
the struggle was intensified, the normal relations of men were
utterly perverted, and a premium was placed on the anti-
social qualities. Thus, it became increasingly difficult to preserve that sanity of judgement and moderation of conduct which
thrive only in time of peace. This fact explains the anomaly of
the fate of Nicias, who despite his one defect, 'an excessive
devotion to divination' (vii. 50), was nevertheless 'of all contemporary Greeks the least worthy to meet with such misfor-
tune, because he had passed his whole life in the cultivation of
conventional virtue' (vii. 86. 5). To suppose that, in his observations either on the fate of Nicias or on that of the unselfish
victims of the plague, Thucydides is contemptuous and cynical
is to betray a complete failure to understand his mind. To
him, as a man of science, the conventional represents successful
adjustment to the more or less permanent physical conditions
of life, and to that extent the normal is the right. The war, by

disrupting those conditions, swept away the norms or standards of conduct painfully erected by men to meet the conditions of peace, and so gave rise to a problem of suffering which science can merely note, but which it is the task of philosophy to justify and explain.

VIII

THE SCIENTIFIC TRADITION AFTER THUCYDIDES

IN the hands of Thucydides history rose to the level of political science; but it has been so common to think of it in other ways that it is only by an effort of mind that one does so in his case. The declension of history from that level must now be studied, if only to emphasize the peculiarity of the position to which it had been elevated by Thucydides, and the invasion of new influences, besides the revival of old ones, in historical composition.

It has been generally recognized that the scientific outlook on the world, characteristic of the fifth century B.C., was confronted with and all but overwhelmed by a powerful philosophic impulse equally characteristic of the fourth. That impulse had a serious repercussion upon the spirit and method of historical composition. Plato, indeed, plays with history both in the *Laws* and elsewhere, but the method by which he approaches the problems of politics is essentially philosophical and, accordingly, in his hands history ceases to be a science. Starting with an *a priori* conception of man and nature, and aiming to present a picture of the world which should be above all things logically coherent, he frequently introduces passages of striking beauty and power, in order to give a pseudo-historical setting to what is really a logical reconstruction; but, as these reconstructions are never based on a close examination of the actual world of $\gamma \acute{\epsilon} \nu \epsilon \sigma \iota s$ and $\phi \theta o \rho \acute{a}$, and are never limited to what may be observed and verified, they represent a reversion to that 'mythical' treatment of history which Thucydides had so sternly denounced. Great, therefore, as may be their philosophic interest and significance, they are in no sense scientific.

Aristotle, while reacting vigorously from the other-worldliness of Plato, was none the less unable to escape completely from the trammels of Platonic method. For example, the treatise on the Athenian constitution, which is the one surviving fragment of purely historical composition attributable to him, appears to embody an attempt to explain and justify the 'middle position' in contemporary Athenian politics, by finding for it respectable antecedents in the work of early reformers, particularly Draco and Solon. So far as this criticism is well-founded, the *Athenian Constitution* would appear to lack the objectivity of a genuine prognosis; and to treat history in this way as 'past politics' would have shocked the scientific spirit of Thucydides as greatly as he would have been shocked by the frankly 'mythical' treatment which it received in the hands of Plato. The *Politics* also, while largely dominated by a sense of the relation of specific ends and means, is nevertheless shot through and through with notions of valuation which really belong to ethics. Consequently, in spite of the fact that Aristotle reveals to the tyrant, the oligarch, and to the constitutional democrat, the specific prescriptions necessary for the preservation of their rule, his interest, like Plato's, lies ultimately in the portrayal of an ideal commonwealth, which shall serve as the spiritual home of the Aristotelian man. So also to him poetry is more 'scientific'[1] (or philosophic) than history, because poetry deals with universals, while history after all represents only the knowledge of particulars; that is to say, it is mere semeiology, and never attains the point of genuine prognosis.

Nevertheless, as we have already pointed out,[2] there is to be found in Aristotle, alongside the philosophic point of view which he inherits from Plato, another point of view which he imports from his scientific studies, and which he shares with Thucydides and with the biological and medical writers of the fifth century. 'We should consider', he says, 'not only what form of government is best, but also what is possible and what is easily attainable by all' (*Pol.* 1288^b 24). From this standpoint, experience rather than dogma becomes the real teacher of mankind; and the value which Aristotle placed on experience is indicated by the tradition that he caused to be made a digest of no less than one hundred and fifty-eight living constitutions as material for the generalizations on political science which he embodied in the *Politics*. If the *Constitution of Athens* is one

[1] See *Mind*, xxxi, no. 124.   [2] Ch. iv, p. 35, above.

of these, then it must be admitted that Aristotle himself violated the principle expressed in the *Poetics*, by which history is relegated to the knowledge of mere particulars. The *Constitution of Athens* is indeed mainly a reconstruction of past events, and generalization is as a rule avoided. Nevertheless it contains occasional observations which clearly exemplify the genuine prognosis, as it was understood by Thucydides, and which illustrate the difficulty of confining history to the simple record of facts. Of these one example may be cited. Speaking of the contemporary democracy, Aristotle says: 'Even the jurisdiction of the Council has passed into the hands of the people at large; and this appears to be a judicious change, *since small bodies are more open to corruption, whether by actual money or by influence, than large ones*' (c. 41. 10). This generalization embodies one of the strongest practical arguments which, under ancient conditions, could be made in favour of democracy.

In his attitude to the practical questions of political science, there is indeed a curious similarity between the views of Aristotle and those of Thucydides. Both, for example, agree in deriving the state from a consolidation of villages, originating to make possible security and concrete well-being; and, although Aristotle, in his anxiety to prove the naturalness of political association, argues that a social instinct is implanted in all men by nature, he nevertheless agrees with Thucydides so far as to admit that the state arises by no spontaneous process, but is the deliberate creation of far-seeing men, the object of which is to associate 'power' with 'justice' or 'might' with 'right'. 'A social instinct is implanted in all men by nature, and yet he who first founded the state was the greatest of all benefactors.'[1] In the argument for inequality, intended to justify that relationship of authority and subjection which expresses itself, economically in the distinction between master and servant, politically in that between ruler and ruled, Aristotle also revives Thucydides' notion regarding the formal character of government. 'Virtue, when furnished with means, may be deemed to have the greatest power of doing violence; and, as superior power is found only where there is superior excellence

[1] *Pol.* 1253ᵃ 29 ὁ δὲ πρῶτος συστήσας μεγίστων ἀγαθῶν αἴτιος.

of some kind, power is thought to imply virtue.'[1] Here we have the use of ἀρετή in the scientific sense, in which for example the word is applied by Thucydides to Antiphon (viii. 68. 1)— a usage with which Bury[2] compares the Machiavellian *virtu*, without perhaps appreciating its full significance as an expression of the scientific attitude which both writers had toward life.

The same parallelism which marks the attitude of Thucydides and Aristotle toward the question of how political relationship is established, marks also their view of how that relationship is maintained. Speaking of the tie which binds master and servant, Aristotle observes that, where the relationship between them is natural, they are friends and have a common interest, but, where it rests merely on law and force, the reverse is the case (1255^b 12). Thus to him, as to Thucydides, it is the perception of a common interest which ensures the maintenance of the economic relationship, and the same is true of the political relationship as well. 'I may begin by assuming, that the portion of the state which desires permanence ought to be stronger than that which desires the reverse' (1296^b 15). On this general principle, it becomes easy to determine the conditions necessary to secure the permanence of oligarchy. 'The nature of those admitted should be such as will make the entire governing body stronger than those who are excluded' (1320^b 28). But what applies to oligarchies applies equally to all states. 'Speaking generally, we may say that, whatever legal enactments are held to be for the interest of states, all these preserve states. And the great preserving principle is the one which has been repeatedly mentioned—to have a care that the loyal citizens should outnumber the disloyal'.[3] Herein lies the significance of the democratic principle of government by consent, the object of which is, as we have said,[4] to ensure that generally speaking, the compulsion of the state shall never be applied where it cannot be made effective. 'Government should rely

---

[1] μὴ ἄνευ ἀρετῆς εἶναι τὴν βίαν.   [2] *Ancient Greek Historians*, p. 145.
[3] 1309^b 17, Jowett's translation; but κρεῖττον, the Greek word, really means *outweigh*, and excludes the notion of merely numerical superiority.
[4] Ch. vii, above.

on itself, and not on foreign aid nor on the good will of a majority of foreign states, but on the *general willingness of all classes* in the state to maintain the constitution' ($1294^b\,35$). This principle indeed gives the greatest assurance of permanence, and constitutes the real vindication of Cleisthenic democracy which, as we have seen, represses no considerable interest within the social whole, but gives adequate, if not equal, expression to them all.

A further point of comparison between Thucydides and Aristotle may perhaps be noted, and that is the preference which Thucydides felt for the middle state even over the state of Periclean Athens, and which Aristotle felt for the 'polity' over all but his own ideal form. 'I do not think the worse of a citizen who takes some thought about his life and his property; for I believe that a man's sense of his own interest will quicken his interest in the prosperity of the state' (Thuc. vi. 9. 2). That this sentiment, which Thucydides puts into the mouth of Nicias, was in reality his own, or at any rate shared by him, is proved by the passage in which, speaking in his own person, he put the stamp of approval upon the so-called government of the Five Thousand, 'the best government during its early days which the Athenians in my lifetime ever experienced' (viii. 97. 2). The reason for this judgement is clear, and it flows from the general view which Thucydides held regarding the nature and function of the state. Failing an ideal form, the government of the Five Thousand was best because it put political power into the hands of the most substantial interest in Attica, and into the hands of those most capable of protecting that interest. We have already noted the preference which Aristotle evidently felt for the middle class. Their virtues he outlined in *Politics*, $1295^a\,25$–$1297^a\,13$; they are, because of the character of their life, the safest and sanest element to be found in Hellas; consequently those constitutions are practically best in which, so to speak, the centre of gravity lies with them.

This consideration suggests a final point of comparison between the two authors. 'The earliest government which existed among the Greeks, after the overthrow of the (patriarchal) monarchy, grew up out of the warrior class, and was originally taken from the Knights, for strength and superiority in war at that time depended on cavalry; indeed, without discipline, infantry are useless, and in ancient times there was no military knowledge or tactics, and therefore the strength of armies lay in their cavalry. But when cities increased, and the heavy-armed grew in strength, more had a share in the government; and this is the reason why the states which we call constitutional governments (or "polities") have been hitherto called democracies. Ancient constitutions, as might be expected, were oligarchical and royal; their population being small, they had no considerable middle class; the people were therefore the more content to be governed' (1297^b 16–28). This is to say, with Thucydides, that government in the last analysis takes its colour from social and economic conditions or, as Thucydides and Hippocrates put it, reflects the physical basis of life. Changes, therefore, in the form and spirit of the state are not dependent upon any metaphysical principle, nor are they brought about in any arbitrary fashion; but the life and death of the state involve the fate of the individuals and groups who compose the political society, and of the manner of life which these from time to time adopt. Hence, for example, the existence of the 'middle state' depends upon the existence of a middle class, and upon the possibility of maintaining such a class amid the peculiar conditions of life existent in the Mediterranean world.

Among the specifically historical authors of the classical period there never arose in Greece a second Thucydides; because, with one notable exception, there was no one who preserved the genuinely scientific method of attack. That exception was the curious unknown, who goes by the name of Old Oligarch, and whose treatise on the *Constitution of Athens* is printed in the collected works of Xenophon. The 'prognosis' of advanced democracy given in that treatise rivals, as it resembles, the work of Thucydides in penetrating analysis. Old Oligarch sweeps to one side the smoke-screen of idealism with which the extreme democrats camouflaged the true nature of their power, and with cool detachment relates the institutions of advanced democracy to its physical basis, offering at the same time a specific prescription for the preservation of this paradise of the sea-faring rabble. But his work after all is a mere sketch.

Xenophon, the first voluminous writer after Thucydides, illustrates in more than one respect a grave declension from the genuinely scientific ideal. The *Hellenica*, his most ambitious work, is generally pronounced to be a dull and uninspired chronicle. The reason for this is clear. Xenophon, while possessing many of the merits of a good chronicler, nevertheless lacks the essential quality of a genuine scientist. He is like the stupid physician, who can see that his patient is ill but cannot tell what is wrong with him; in short, he lacks the insight necessary for correct prognosis. So also, in the *Anabasis*, while he reveals in his colourful picture of the expedition of the Ten Thousand, a power of presentation as brilliant as it is fascinating, he fails apparently to appreciate the real significance of this expedition for the relations of Greek and Persian, and it was left for others to visualize the possibilities revealed by that romantic adventure. Polybius notes that it was Philip of Macedon who estimated the situation, and was preparing to act upon it, when death cut short his career and transferred the task to Alexander (Polyb. iii. 6. 12). Xenophon himself was indeed a sort of knight-errant, with one eye fixed on excitement and the other on the prospect of booty. His true strength lay in those ideal characterizations of men and events which combine the atmosphere of the days of chivalry with the moralizings of the fairy tale.

The works of the historians of the fourth and third centuries survive merely in fragments, or not at all; and so it is impossible to characterize them with justice. It may, however, be gathered that the vast disturbances which transformed a half-barbarous feudal chieftain into the captain-general of Hellas, and then made him monarch of the civilized world, at once the champion and avenger of Hellenism and the heir and successor of the King of Kings, offered no great inspiration to historians, but served merely as the occasion of partial narratives and biographies of individuals, or as the inspiration of the first of those ponderous universal histories whose authors displayed an appetite for facts equalled only by their incapacity to digest them. This is the general impression derived from the references to his predecessors contained in Polybius, whose judgement is always severe and, in the case at least of Timaeus, possibly malicious. Nevertheless, it is perhaps worth while to recall briefly certain of his criticisms in order to illustrate as far as possible the leading features of historical composition, and the influences which were predominant among the authors of that time.

Of these influences one of the most significant was undoubtedly that of rhetoric. According to Dionysius of Halicarnassus, Ephorus and Theopompus were the only historical authors whose diction was accurate and finished. This criticism, coming from such a source, is in itself ominous. Both of them students in the school of Isocrates, and Theopompus at least the winner of a prize for oratory, they had each mastered the 'Art' which concerns itself not with the establishment of truth but with the means of persuasion, and which in consequence possesses much greater affinities with imaginative literature than it does with history. For while to history the fact is sacred, the object of rhetoric, like that of poetry, is achieved if the presentation is 'convincing'. The facts of history may be difficult to establish, as the evidence for them is obscure or deficient; this, however, constitutes no excuse for the deliberate perversion of facts with the object of producing a plausible story. Thus scientific presumption is sharply distinguished from that kind of 'probability' upon which the attention of rhetoricians was concentrated and with which alone they were concerned.

Isocrates is said to have remarked of his two pupils 'that while Ephorus required the spur, Theopompus needed the bit'. This criticism would seem to be confirmed by the observations of Polybius upon these authors; for, while he makes no comment on the style of Ephorus, he specifically accuses Theopompus of an extravagance of language which reaches the point of self-contradiction, besides being coarse and unbecoming to the dignity of history (Polyb. viii. 9–11). This extravagance he illustrates from the judgement passed by Theopompus on Philip of Macedon. Europe, says Theopompus, had never

before produced such a man as Philip, and yet he was so in-
continent that he ruined his own home, and so addicted to
drink that he was frequently seen by his friends intoxicated in
broad daylight. His friends and companions were worse brutes
and of a more beastly disposition than the Centaurs or the
Laestregones, or any other monsters. Are these the men, asks
Polybius, who by their bravery, industry, and virtue raised
Macedonia from the status of a petty kingdom to that of the most
glorious monarchy in the world? The quotation seems indeed to
reveal, not so much a paradox in the character of Philip and his
friends, as the danger which lurks for the historian in the tricks
of rhetoric, whether that of the balanced sentence or that of the
simile.

It cannot be said that Thucydides himself was wholly immune
from the influence of rhetoric which, invented to serve the
needs of democracy at Syracuse and thence spreading through
the city states of Sicily, had invaded Athens at least as early
as 427 B.C. In that year Gorgias of Leontini, head of the
deputation which came to seek aid for his native city against
Syracuse, had startled and delighted the Athenians by a magni-
ficent display of the 'Art'. In so doing, he provided not merely
a demonstration of unusual skill in the arrangement and
presentation of ideas, but also a revelation of the knowledge
which he possessed of human psychology—a knowledge the
value of which was proved by the fact that it worked. Students
of Thucydides have always been impressed by the close
analogy between his psychological views and those of the
sophists; and a cursory examination of either the *Epitaphius* or
the *Encomium on Helen* is sufficient to prove the direct influence
which Gorgias must have exercised upon his style of composition. Yet these considerations do not prove that Thucydides
ever succumbed to the great danger of rhetoric, that of sacrific-
ing truth to the exigencies of style. To him, as we have seen,
the facts were sacred (Thuc. i. 22), and so, unless there is
reason for questioning his own positive statement, the narrative
portion of his work escapes the imputation of rhetorical
influence. With regard to the speeches, we may observe from
at least one example the vast difference between the spirit

of Thucydides' treatment and that of a man who, in handling the same theme, is frankly rhetorical.

Polybius (xii. 25k–26), criticizing Timaeus, remarks that of all those who held power in Sicily after the death of the elder Gelo, among the most capable were Hermocrates, Timoleon, and Pyrrhus of Epirus, and that these are the last persons imaginable to whom one should attribute childish or idle speeches. But Timaeus says that, when Eurymedon came to Sicily (424 B.C.) and was urging the towns to pursue the war against Syracuse, the Geloans, who were in dire straits, sent to Camarina begging for a truce. Hence arose the conference of Gela, consisting of delegates from all the Sicilian states, who came together to discuss terms of peace and the general interests of all concerned. We have already mentioned the address which Thucydides attributes to Hermocrates on that occasion (Thuc. iv. 59–64). It was an argument for reconciliation as a means of warding off the Athenian peril; and, after a sentence or two in which the speaker alludes to the blessings of peace, he breaks off to proceed with the main argument: 'but it is unnecessary to dilate on the blessings of peace any more than on the miseries of war' (62. 2). Compare this with the treatment which the same subject received from Timaeus, as his words are reported by Polybius.[1] 'In the first place he thinks it proper to remind the council that men are aroused in the morning in war time by the trumpet and in peace by the crowing of cocks. After this he tells them that Heracles founded the Olympian games and truce as a proof of his real preference, and that he had injured all those he fought with under compulsion and by order, but that he had done no evil to any man of his own free will. Next he says that Homer represents Zeus as displeased with Ares and saying:

> Of all the gods who tread the spangled skies,
> Thou most unjust, most odious to our eyes!
> Inhuman discord is thy dire delight,
> The waste of slaughter, and the rage of fight;

---

[1] The translations of Polybius are in general those of W. R. Paton, Loeb Classical Library.

that similarly the wisest of his heroes says:

> Cursed is the man, and void of law and right,
> Unworthy property, unworthy light,
> Unfit for public rule, or private care,
> That wretch, that monster, who delights in war.'

Then after reinforcing the same sentiment by a lengthy quotation from Euripides, Hermocrates proceeds to add some arguments of his own. 'War', he declares, 'very much resembles sickness, and peace health, for peace restores even the sick, and in war even the healthy perish. In peace again the old are buried by the young as is natural, while in war it is the reverse, and above all in war there is no safety even up to the walls, but in peace there is safety as far as the boundaries of the land . . .' (ch. 26). Thus, says Polybius (ch. 25 k. 10), the Timaean Hermocrates devotes the greater part of his speech to a matter which does not require a single word, and employs such arguments as none could believe to have been used by any ordinary schoolboy, not to speak of the leading statesman of Syracuse.

Rhetoric, which in the fifth century had belonged to the market place, was in later times relegated to the schools and libraries. This was the consequence, partly of the emasculation of civic life due to the subjugation of Hellas, partly of the steadily increasing complexity of affairs, which necessitated specialization. For similar reasons, the writing of history fell into the hands of professionals, and these, if Ephorus and Theopompus may be taken as examples, were often men who, wearied by the emptiness of school declamations, sought to practise their art in the more promising and profitable field of historical composition. Thus Polybius, in the second century, was a voice crying in the wilderness, when he deplored the extinction of that splendid amateurism which had produced the great writers of classical Greece, but which had vanished with the society to which it belonged. There is something in his complaint against the mere arm-chair historian, who in the nature of things is forced to discuss matters of which he has no personal experience, and whose knowledge of life is bounded by the four walls of the library. The sin of ignorance he imputes in some degree even to Ephorus (xii. 25 f.), but the classical example of this offence is to him the polymath Timaeus who, having buried himself for nearly fifty years in the library at Athens, 'considered himself peculiarly qualified to write history, making herein a great mistake' (xii. 25 d).

It is impossible to follow in detail the criticism which Polybius launches against Timaeus (xii). He accuses him of being a deliberate liar and an unscrupulous knave, guilty of inaccurate and false statements and of judgements darkened by prejudice and perverted by pedantry, while at the same time making a special parade of accuracy and care. Furthermore he alleges that the pronouncements of Timaeus are full of dreams, prodigies, and incredible tales, thoroughly vitiated by craven superstition and womanish love of the marvellous. All these faults he illustrates and, while it must be left to the critic to estimate, in general, the justice of his charges, we may perhaps note one passage in which he endeavours to hold the balance between Timaeus and Aristotle. Aristotle had apparently made some observations upon the Sicilian Locri which Timaeus considered it his duty to refute. In his efforts to do so, he resorts to misrepresentation and personal abuse, falsely imputing outrageous statements to Aristotle, and denouncing him as a pedantic and detestable sophist, who had locked up his surgeon's shop to force his way into every court and on to every stage, and who was a glutton and epicure, catering in everything to his belly. As for the points at issue, Polybius settles them in favour of Aristotle, asserting that his reconstruction of Locrian history is more probable than that of Timaeus (xii. 5). The controversy itself, however, was not so important as the spirit in which it was waged by Timaeus, and Polybius was probably justified in denouncing him for having introduced into history the methods and atmosphere of the agora or of the comic stage. Of this he would never have been guilty had he possessed any real experience (24. 6). His dogmatic assurance was the product of his training, and it, like his methods of controversy, would hardly have survived the vicissitudes of active life.

The triumph of the tendencies just noted marked the failure of history to maintain the standards set for it by Thucydides.

In the hands of romancers, or of professional rhetoricians and literary artists, it could not provide real instruction for serious students of life and politics. Yet, if Polybius is to be believed, a worse fate still was in store for history, which, with Phylarchus a writer of the third century B.C., descended to the level of mere journalism. The aim of Phylarchus was apparently to be sensational, and he sought to gratify the perverted tastes of his readers by making history a medium for the portrayal of all forms of crime, immorality, and treachery, 'as though it were rather the proper function of history to chronicle the commission of sins than to call attention to right and honourable actions, or as if it were less improving to read of that good conduct which we should emulate than of that criminal conduct which we should shun' (ii. 56–61). In Phylarchus, indeed, we have an example of that realism, falsely so called, which is akin to the pseudo-realism of the modern yellow press, or the contemporary 'shocker', the object of which is achieved if it produces a thrill.

Philinus of Agrigentum and Fabius Pictor of Rome may have been innocent of the faults specified above; but each in his own way administered a blow to scientific history no less serious than those which have been recorded. They wrote, says Polybius, 'like lovers', and so in their hands history became propaganda in favour either of Carthage or of Rome. Thus national bias entered in as a final factor to pervert truth, and history was at last reduced to the condition of a living creature incapacitated by the loss of its eyes (i. 14–15 and xii. 12. 3). With this final criticism we may leave the predecessors of Polybius and turn to a consideration of Polybius himself.

Himself a statesman and man of affairs, Polybius, like his father Lycortas, had been involved in the politics of the Achaean league during the period of the Roman protectorate— the half century intervening between the emancipation of Hellas from Macedonian domination and its final subjection to Roman sway. For many years he had been a leader of the moderate nationalists; and, as such, he had sought to mediate between the views of those who would have involved Greece in a fatal conflict for independence, and those who desired to

knowledge to deal properly with circumstances as they arise' (iii. 7. 6–7).

So far Polybius appears to have revived scientific conceptions, once more, so to speak, bringing history down from heaven to earth, and making possible an examination of causes which, while it may not be exhaustive, is at any rate fruitful, so far as it goes. Upon the study of these he lays the greatest possible emphasis. For him, indeed, they constitute the heart and soul of historical research. Thus, for example, he warns both writers and readers of history to pay attention not merely to the actual narrative of facts, but to what precedes, what accompanies, and what follows each event (iii. 31. 11–12). 'For if we take from history the discussion of why, how, and wherefore each thing was done, and whether the result was what we should reasonably have expected, what is left is but a clever essay and not a lesson and, while pleasing for the moment, it is of no possible benefit for the future.' On the other hand 'the peculiar function of history is to discover, in the first place, the words actually spoken, whatever they were, and next to ascertain the reason (αἰτία) why what was done or spoken led to failure or success. For the mere statement of a fact may interest us, but is in no sense serviceable. When, however, we add the cause of it, the study of history becomes fruitful. For it is the mental transference of similar circumstances to our own times that gives us the means of forming an anticipation of what is about to happen[1] and enables us . . . to face with more confidence the difficulties which menace us'. It was this conviction which determined for Polybius at once the scope and limitations of his work, and, at the same time, imposed upon him a standard of relevance without which he could hardly have dealt with so vast a theme.

In the passage just quoted, there are two points worthy of remark. Firstly, Polybius affirms the sanctity of the fact in such a way as to exclude even speeches like those in Thucydides. The convention by which an author was permitted to put his own interpretation into the mouths of others, he specifically branded as illegitimate, no doubt because it lent

[1] xii. 25^b 3, ἀφορμαὶ καὶ προλήψεις εἰς τὸ προϊδέσθαι τὸ μέλλον.

itself so readily to abuse.[1] Secondly, his reference to the possibility of the mental transfer of circumstances from one period to another implies belief in the stability of human nature in relation to the environment, an assumption which lies at the very foundation of scientific history. Without this assumption experience is meaningless. If it be granted, the past at once acquires significance, and it becomes correct to describe history as the memory of humanity, fulfilling the same function in the life of the race as memory in the life of the individual.

The emphasis which Polybius lays on the study of causes raises the question: what does he mean by an historical cause? To this question he himself offers an answer. There are some, he declares, who overlook the great and essential distinction between the immediate occasion (ἀρχή) and the true cause and purpose (αἰτία καὶ πρόφασις), the latter being the first origin of all, and the occasion coming last. 'By the occasion of anything, I mean the first attempt to execute and put in action plans on which we have decided; by its causes, those factors which inspire our judgements and opinions, to wit, our notions of things, our states of mind, our reasonings about this, in short everything through which we are led to make decisions and plans' (iii. 6, 7). This, it may be granted, is a large field, and within it there will be room for difference of opinion as to whether or not he is right in attributing particular events to particular causes. He himself is fully conscious of the difficulty of his task, especially in view of the magnitude of his work, and the consequent necessity of comprehensive treatment (xvi. 20. 8, 9). Nevertheless, it can hardly be questioned that in seeking for the causes of events in the purposes which from time to time governed the various peoples, and the sources of strength on which they relied in their dealings with one another, he was at least looking in the right place (i. 3. 9).

The task which he set himself was to describe and account for the process by which the states of the Mediterranean were brought together under the hegemony of Rome (i. 1 and 2; iii. 3, &c.). Mommsen considers that, in spite of certain obvious weaknesses which, from the modern point of view, disfigure

---

[1] Cf. i. 14. 5; ii. 56. 9; xxxviii. 4. 5 and 8, &c.

his work, he has been, generally speaking, successful in his aim. 'To him all subsequent generations, and we too, owe the best part of our knowledge of the Roman development.'[1] 'His books are like the sun in the field of Roman history; at the point where they begin the veil of night which still envelops the Samnite and Pyrrhic wars is raised, and at the point where they end a new and if possible still more vexatious twilight begins.'[2] From this judgement it is, on the whole, impossible to dissent.

The scope of Polybius' work makes it impossible for us to attempt any detailed analysis; but it may be suggested that his real strength lies in his appreciation of the interconnexion of events, 'how the Romans dealt with each contingency as it arose' (iii. 3. 9), and 'what particular circumstances obstructed their grand design, or again, how and at what time circumstances contributed to its execution' (viii. 2. 6). Thus, for example, he makes the whole movement toward world conquest turn upon the Hannibalic war, perceiving the critical significance of that struggle as an effort to reverse the decision of the First Punic war and re-establish Carthaginian control over the western Mediterranean. The First Punic war had been occasioned by the fear lest, if the mistress of Italy should allow the Carthaginians to close the straits of Messina, she would imperil her newly won Italian hegemony; but it had soon developed into a conflict for the control of Sicily, the issue of which could be decided only by sea power. Thus Rome was led to dispute with Carthage command of the sea; and this, once secured, brought her into relations with the Greek states of the Adriatic seaboard, and with the Macedonian monarchy (i and ii). But the Carthaginians, although defeated, had not been crushed. They had come to terms under pressure of circumstances, but their spirit had not been broken (iii. 12. 5). Furthermore, in the fact that the Romans had taken advantage of their domestic troubles to seize Sardinia, they had experienced not merely a deep humiliation but also a sense of the peril to which their empire was exposed by the loss of sea power. Thus, under the leadership of Hamilcar Barca and of his greater son, they were

[1] Mommsen, *History of Rome*, iv. 242.
[2] Op. cit., p. 247.

inspired to repair their shattered fortunes by building up a new empire in Spain. The Second Punic war was therefore a war of revenge, and the Carthaginians, when they felt themselves ready, embarked with confidence upon the struggle, although, because of their maritime inferiority, they were forced to undertake the hazardous enterprise of attacking Rome by land (iii. 9. 6–10). For this design they were indebted to Hannibal, to whose genius they also committed its execution; and whatever degree of success attended the venture was due to him (ix. 22. 1; xi. 19). 'Such a great and wonderful product of nature is a man whose mind is properly endowed by its original constitution to execute any project within human power' (ix. 22. 6). To Hannibal also the Carthaginians owed the advice to accept such terms as the Romans offered after their final defeat at Zama (xv. 18, 19). His perception enabled him to realize that the measure of relative strength had been taken, and that, so far as Carthage was concerned, there was no further possibility of disputing the claim of Rome to dominate the Mediterranean.

For Rome, on the other hand, the war had meant that the chief and most essential step in their scheme of universal aggression had been taken, and the Romans were thus emboldened to reach out their hands and grasp the rest and to cross with an army to Greece and Asia (i. 3. 6). The Greeks had watched the issue that was being settled in Italy with deep interest and apprehension. 'If we wait for those clouds that loom in the west to settle on Hellas, I very much fear lest we may all of us find this game of truces and wars that we play so rudely interrupted that we shall be fain to pray to the gods to give us still the power of fighting with each other and of making peace when we will, the power in a word of settling our differences by ourselves' (v. 104. 10 and 11). Thus Philip of Macedon and the leading statesmen of Greece ceased henceforth, in their dealings with one another, to base their action on events in Greece, but the eyes of all were turned on the issues in Italy.[1] At the outbreak of the war Philip had already decided to build a fleet (v. 109), but his timidity lost him the

---

[1] v. 105. 3; 217 B.C.

chance of entering the Adriatic and subduing Illyria (v. 110. 9;
216 B.C.). The subsequent alliance which he made with
Hannibal (vii. 9) marked his sense of the danger to be apprehended from the Romans, and committed him, upon the conclusion of the Hannibalic war, to a contest with them for the
control of the Adriatic and of peninsular Greece, a contest
which decided once and for all the superiority of the Roman
legion over the Macedonian phalanx (xviii. 28–33). The con-
querors were satisfied to strip the king of his navy, and force
him to repudiate his claim to dominate the Greek states; but,
conscious of the barbarian peril on the north (ii. 35. 5 foll.)
and of the usefulness of Macedonia as a buffer against the
barbarians (xviii. 37. 9), they left Philip with sufficient power
to discharge the historic mission of his country. Thus Polybius
describes the beginnings of Roman intervention in the east, and
the initiation of the policy of ensuring a balance of power which
dictated also her attitude towards Syria, Egypt, and the minor
states of Europe and Asia. Likewise he describes the break-
down of that policy which began with the revolt of Perseus
(xxviii. 10; xxix. 5, &c.) and culminated in the direct extension
of imperial administration over Macedonia and Greece, as in
the next century it was ultimately extended over the whole
Mediterranean basin. Throughout he appears to cling to
physical principles of interpretation, the conflict of human
wills and purposes in relation to concrete interests which men
visualized, and for the realization of which they contended or
co-operated with one another.

The same principles appear, on the whole, to have governed
his treatment of individuals. We have already noticed his
estimate of Hannibal, the first of those great captains who,
after Alexander, dominated the stage of European history. In
his judgement of the character and career of Scipio Africanus,
he offers an illustration of the same principles of interpretation,
interesting because of their application to an individual whose
influence had been so great, and with whose family circle the
author himself was so intimately associated. Scipio was one
of the first great personalities to emerge in Roman history.
Because of the magnitude of his achievements, he was popularly

regarded as a super-man, in whom the masses saw, so to speak,
an incarnation of Fortune herself, and, apparently, he was not
unwilling to capitalize the general impression (x. 11). In point
of fact, however, his real strength lay, like that of Themistocles
and Pericles, in his essentially human qualities. 'He was',
declares Polybius, 'kind and munificent and agreeable in his
address. He reckoned on his popularity with the masses and,
by making his actions conform to the actual sentiment of the
people, and of his mother, he not only attained his objects,
but was believed to have acted under a sort of divine inspiration.
For those who are incapable of taking an accurate view of
opportunities, causes, and dispositions, either from lack of
natural ability (διὰ φαυλότητα φύσεως) or from inexperience and
ignorance, attribute to the gods and to fortune the causes of
what is accomplished by shrewdness and with calculation and
foresight.'[1]

We may thus conclude that Polybius, both in his perception
of the causal connexion of events and in his conception of the
part which individuals play in bringing those events to pass,
revives the genuinely scientific tradition and writes in a manner
not unworthy of the greatest of his predecessors. Not satisfied,
however, to remain at this level of interpretation, and seeking
to probe more deeply into the sources of Roman power, he
attributes the qualities of the Romans to their constitution and,
in a well-known passage (Book VI), embarks on an elaborate
analysis of the whole institutional environment of Rome. The
result has been unfortunate for his reputation. Mommsen,[2] in
his comment, declares that 'there is hardly a more foolish
speculation than that which derives the excellent constitution
of Rome from a judicious mixture of monarchical, aristocratic,
and democratic elements, and deduces the successes of Rome
from the excellence of her constitution'. Bury also[3] protests
against a theory which finds 'the secret of life in a mechanical
adjustment of the parts of the state'.

From these judgements it is difficult to dissent. The actual

---

[1] x. 5. 6–8 τὰς αἰτίας τῶν δι' ἀγχίνοιαν καὶ ἐκ λογισμοῦ ⟨καὶ⟩ προνοίας ἐπιτελου-
μένων.   [2] Op. cit., p. 247.
[3] *Ancient Greek Historians*, p. 207.

model of the mixed constitution was probably Sparta, and the
theory seems to have been enunciated first by Hippodamus,
the architect of Piraeus, some time in the course of the fifth
century.[1] Subsequently, after an uncertain history, it was
adopted and developed by Dicaearchus and the third century
Stoics, to be taken over from them by Polybius, who passed it
on in turn to Cicero and the eulogists of the English constitution in the eighteenth century.[2] In the hands of Polybius this
theory appears in connexion with the theory of cycles, and serves
to explain how, in the unique case of Rome, the normal course
of cyclical evolution was retarded, and a temporary equilibrium
was secured. Now the theory of cycles had been uncritically
accepted by Polybius 'from Plato and certain other philosophers', as he himself specifically admits (vi. 5. 1). Its object
was to provide a ready and easy way of forecasting the future
of states. 'Such', says Polybius, concluding his statement of
the theory, 'is the cycle of political revolution, the course
appointed by nature in which constitutions change, disappear,
and finally return to the point from which they started. Any-
one who clearly perceives this may indeed be wrong in his
estimate of the time the process will take, but if his judgement
is untainted by animosity or jealousy he will seldom be mistaken
as to the stage of growth or decline it has reached, and as to
the form into which it will change' (vi. 9. 10–11). Such over-
simplification of the problem, however intriguing, is unquestionably fallacious. Polybius himself admits that it fails to
explain the course of development either in Athens or Thebes,
and he therefore excludes both these as 'abnormal'. The truth
is that the theory of cycles is metaphysical and logical and that,
in deserting the physical bases of explanation, it abandons the
sole foundation upon which genuinely scientific prognostication
may be made. Furthermore, in the case of Rome, it is unnecessary. So far as the state embodied an equilibrium, that
equilibrium can best be understood as reflecting the various
social and economic forces which found expression through the
political machinery. And if, in the time of Polybius, equili-

[1] Newman, *The Politics of Aristotle*, i. 382, foll.; ii. pp. xii–xiii.
[2] Op. cit., i. 264.

brium was threatened, this was because the social revolution following the wars of conquest had corrupted the aristocracy, created a new financial class, and threatened with extinction the peasant farmers who constituted the bone and sinew of the state. This was obvious to the circle with which he was associated, and it is surprising that it did not dawn upon Polybius.

Polybius is on stronger ground when he forgets his theory of cycles, and passes on to a consideration of the actual constitution of Rome. Both this, and the account of the Roman military system which follows it, contain many shrewd observations, which serve largely to redeem his analysis from puerility, and to explain how the Italian federation withstood the fierce and sustained onslaughts of Hannibal. In particular we may note his comment on the function of religion in maintaining the cohesion of the Roman state, while at the same time discounting the shallowness which explains the religious sentiment as mere social cement, consciously adopted by superior people for the sake of the commons, who must be held in check by invisible terrors (vi. 56. 6–13). In order to be scientific it is not necessary to be irreligious, but the duty of the scientist is fulfilled if, without seeking to explain away either the religious or the moral sentiments, he demonstrates the part which these play in sustaining or otherwise the fabric of the state.

A final question remains to be discussed in our examination of Polybius, and that is this: what was his real view of that Fortune (or τύχη) to which he frequently alludes, and of the part which it played in determining the course of human affairs? On this question it must be admitted that he speaks with a certain ambiguity, due no doubt to a conflict between his impulses as a scientist and the religious views which he inherited from the Stoics, and which he was in constant danger of importing into his interpretation of history.

With regard to the general doctrine of causality, there are to be found in Polybius certain passages in which he speaks apparently without equivocation. 'Without a cause, nothing, whether normal or apparently abnormal, can be brought about' (ii. 38. 5). This is a clear affirmation of the scientific position.

This position is implied again in the passage in which he declares his belief that Roman expansion was due to natural causes. 'The progress of the Romans was not due to chance (τύχη) nor was it spontaneous (αὐτομάτως), as some of the Greeks choose to think, but it was eminently probable (ἀλλὰ καὶ λίαν εἰκότως) that they, with the schooling which they had undergone in such vast enterprises, should not merely have aspired to universal dominion, but actually have achieved their aim' (i. 63. 9).

With these passages we may compare the speech of an ambassador, probably delivered in 207 B.C. as a warning to the Aetolians, lest relying on the hope of Roman backing they should involve themselves in war with Philip, and thus provoke the intervention of the Romans in Greece (xi. 4-6). 'War', declares the speaker, 'is like a conflagration. Once we have set the fuel alight the consequences are not within our discretion (ἐπὶ τῇ προαιρέσει) but it spreads wherever chance (τύχη) directs it, guided chiefly by the wind and by the rapidity with which the fuel it feeds on is consumed; often strangely enough (παραλόγως) turning on the very man who lit it . . . at times it destroys its authors, at times advances blindly, bringing unmerited destruction on everything it encounters,[1] ever revived and ever blown anew into a blaze, as if by winds, by the folly of those who approach it. Further, this war in particular is not merely unprofitable, as every war for the most part is, but inglorious as well, and full of dishonour and reproach to its authors. The moment you involve yourselves in conflict with Philip, the threat of Roman intervention becomes acute. Possibly you should have foreseen all the consequences from the beginning, but, as much of the future escapes human foresight, it should be your duty now at last, when these occurrences have opened your eyes to facts, to take better counsel for the future.'

In this interesting utterance, which Polybius quotes with approval, we may detect a certain ambiguity. It may be questioned whether the speaker thinks of τύχη, in the spirit of Thucydides, simply as the incalculable element in human affairs or whether he visualizes it as an active power, which interferes for its own purpose with the natural order. The same

[1] ἀδίκως φθείρων: cf. the fate of Nicias.

ambiguity is evident when he speaks of the Roman empire as
the most marvellous of all the achievements of Fortune (i. 1–4
and viii. 2), or when he quotes as inspired the utterance of
Demetrius of Phalerum on the fall of Persia and the rise of
Macedon, in which he sees 'the cruelty of Fortune, who . . .
never compacts with life, but always defeats our reckoning
by some novel stroke, demonstrating her power by foiling our
expectations . . . and now making it clear to all men that, by
endowing the Macedonians with all the wealth of Persia, she
has but lent them those blessings until she decides to deal
differently with them' (xxix. 21). This prophecy, notes Polybius, was confirmed within fifty-three years by the fall of the
monarchy of Macedon, 'so that in pronouncing on this and
similar phenomena we may well say that the thing was a heaven-
sent infatuation, and that all the Macedonians were visited by
the wrath of God' (xxxvi. 17. 15). He may indeed say so, but
to introduce such a judgement into an historical work is to
number oneself among the prophets, and to overrun the
limitations of scientific method.

There is one passage (xxxvi. 17) which is of critical importance as revealing the views of Polybius with regard to the question of divine intervention in human affairs. 'As for matters',
he says, 'the efficient and final cause of which it is possible to
discover, we should not, I think, put them down to divine
action', citing as an example the decline of the birth-rate in
Greece. . . . 'But as regards things the causes of which it is
impossible or difficult for a mere man to understand, we may
perhaps be justified in . . . setting them down to the action of
a god or chance. I mean such things as exceptionally heavy
and continuous rain or snow or, on the other hand, the destruction of crops by severe drought or frost, or a persistent outbreak of plague, or other similar things of which it is not easy
to detect the cause.'

Commenting on this and other passages in which Polybius
refers to Fortune, Bury[1] declares that, having originally started
with the conception of an extra-natural power, directing the
world and diverting the course of events from its natural path,

[1] Op. cit., p. 203.

Polybius was led by wider experience of life and deeper study of history to reduce within narrower and narrower bounds the intervention of this *deus ex machina*, until he finally reached the view that it was superfluous for the pragmatical historian. It is difficult to find evidence which would support this view. Polybius began his work in middle life by pronouncing the Roman empire to be the most marvellous achievement of Fortune; he concluded it in old age with a prayer to the same Fortune that she might spare him to enjoy a few years of peace and happiness on his native soil before his bones were finally laid to rest (xxxix. 8). Furthermore, the implication of Bury's view is, we think, unsound, and betrays a failure to understand what scientific history really is. Whatever may be the character of an author's religious and philosophic principles is quite immaterial, so long as he keeps them out of the picture. The question is, as the author of *Ancient Medicine* has declared, entirely one of method, whether or not it is legitimate to admit the general hypothesis. We may grant that in his actual reconstruction of events and causes, Polybius made little or no use of the general hypothesis; and that is what gives scientific value to his work. Nevertheless, it is clear that on the question of method his views were unsound. The truth is that, in his view of historical causation, he carries us back to the days of Herodotus. So far as he was concerned, the methodological principles of fifth-century science might never have been laid down; and the example which Thucydides had given of their application to history was likewise without significance.

IX
CONCLUSION

IT has been frequently asserted that the conception of scientific history was a product of the nineteenth century. If, however, our argument is valid, it must be admitted that, already in the fifth century B.C., Thucydides had grasped and applied the principles of scientific method with such success that his work constitutes a standard of presentation. From that standard, as we have seen, even his immediate successors fell short, and throughout the whole Graeco-Roman period there was no one who rivalled him either in the assurance with which he grasped the method or in the skill with which he applied it, with the one possible exception of St. Augustine, who probably derived his canons of interpretation, indirectly, from Thucydides himself. The unchallenged reign of absolutes, which succeeded the collapse of the Graeco-Roman world, and for a thousand years dominated the thought of men, necessarily involved the eclipse of scientific history, which was destined to re-appear only in the more congenial atmosphere of the Renaissance. From that day to our own the concern of historians has been to perfect their methodology and, as they have succeeded in doing so, they have approached once more the standard set by Thucydides. For history becomes scientific in so far as it observes the strict limitations of method imposed upon it by him, and guards itself not merely against the danger of importing the artifices of rhetoric, but also against the more subtle peril of admitting those religious or metaphysical canons of interpretation which were known to the Hippocratics as the 'general hypothesis', and to Thucydides as the 'mythical'. These being excluded, the scientific historian is left merely with the concept of a natural order of which man, like the environment, forms a part, and his problem is to exhibit the relationships which from time to time develop among men in contact with the environmental world. Such relationships being, *ex hypothesi*, uniform and regular, the study of them yields those generalizations about human action which constitute the usefulness of history and give to it the character of science.

There are some, however, who demand of history that it should furnish predictions as certain and definite as those of natural science and, unless it does so, they refuse to call it scientific. In other words, they require that it should make possible not merely the formulation of general principles but the actual forecasting of events. In the present condition of human knowledge their demand is vain; and, despite the growing importance of statistical methods, it is likely for some time to remain so. The Romans, oppressed by the tyranny of the empire, were fond of inquiring when relief might be expected. To that question history returned no answer; and to get a reply they were forced to resort to astrology, which was a kind of metaphysics. Plato also, desiring to find a scheme by which he might be enabled to predict the future of states, adopted the theory of cycles; but, in so doing, he rationalized his account of the cycle of evolution to such a degree as to make it inapplicable to actual societies, the life of which is rooted in the 'physical' constitution. The same difficulty attends more modern attempts to pierce the veil of the future. Thus history does not afford ground for specific predictions; nor is it just to require that the 'laws' of history should be valid in the same sense and to the same degree as those of the sciences in which it is possible, by isolating the materials, to subject the 'laws' to experimental verification.

We have said that history possesses a scientific character in so far as it yields useful generalizations about human action or, in other words, enables us to 'prognosticate' in any given situation with reasonable assurance of finding ourselves correct. Of such prognostications, the numerous examples which Thucydides offers are evidence of the deep understanding with which he watched the pageant of humanity. Nevertheless, his merit lies not so much in the fact that he illustrated the nature of prognosis, but rather in the fact that he revealed for the first time the limits within which it might legitimately be made. For while a deeper study of human nature and a fuller know-

ledge of the environmental world doubtless afford assurance
of real improvement in the quality of historical interpretation,
nevertheless Thucydides can hardly be denied the credit of
having first directed attention to the concepts, the use of which
makes progress possible. His true greatness, therefore, is that
of a pioneer in scientific method.

For, revelation apart, there is no source but experience to
which men may turn for direction; and thus it is that the
formulations of experience—the generalizations or prognostications of history—serve to guide their footsteps along the dark
pathway of life, 'causing them', as Polybius observes, 'to face
with greater confidence the difficulties which menace them'.
To those whose temperament demands the assurance of an
absolute revelation this truth may seem abhorrent; and, repelled
by the manifest deficiencies of the world of sense, they will
prefer to take refuge in a world of the imagination which they
are free to construct for themselves according to the dictates of
poetic justice. To those, however, who are content to accept
the world as it is, and to walk by faith, the work of Thucydides
and of scientists like him will appear anything but useless.
Repudiating as false the notion that history teaches nothing,
they will nevertheless refrain from any attempt to find in it
a manifestation of the workings of Providence, or a realization
of the Idea, or any other religious or metaphysical principle.
But accepting the postulate of a stable constitution both of
man and of nature, and looking for the causes of historical
events in modifications of the stimuli to which men are exposed,
they will content themselves with formulating such uniformities
as they may observe, while in the case of those occurrences
which do not yield to prognosis, they will consign them, either
with Thucydides, to the realm of the 'incalculable', or with his
modern successors, as for example Darwin, to that of 'accident'.

It thus appears that science, if it is anything, is simply a way
of looking at the world, and we may add that the flights of
science are taken on the wings of faith. In seeking for uniformities in the constitution of man and nature, science starts
with the conviction that such uniformities are therein to be
found. But there is no means of proving that this is the case,

and thus demonstrating to an unbeliever that historical prognostication is useful or even possible. It may be urged that men
do as a fact regulate their lives largely on this assumption;
but certainly no number of successful prognostications would
suffice to demonstrate the ultimate truth of the postulate, the
acceptance of which is the precondition of prognosis itself.
All that can be done, then, is to apply the pragmatic test, and
illustrate the fruits of the scientific method in comparison with
the methods adopted by others, and this is what, in the case of
Thucydides, we have attempted to do. But at those moments
when scientific faith is weak, men will inevitably revert to other
views of history, as they did in the century following Thucydides.

Because of the rigour with which he observes the limitations
of his self-imposed method, it is vain to look in Thucydides for
any positive statement of his beliefs. Nevertheless, we have
protested at least against the opinion of Bury that Thucydides
was a cynic,[1] and that protest we now venture to reiterate. The
charge of cynicism might indeed be levelled with much more
justice against Bury himself; for in reducing[2] the causes of the
fall of the Roman empire to a 'series of contingent events', and
formally affirming that 'no general causes can be assigned' for
that catastrophe, Bury in effect denies the possibility of prognosis, and betrays his complete lack of faith in the intelligibility
of human history. With this judgement it is impossible to think
that Thucydides would have agreed. It was Thucydides who
first laid down the distinction between the 'occasion' and the
'true cause', and who taught historians to look from the one
to the other for the real explanation of events. In so doing, he
dissociated himself from cynicism and all the philosophic
nihilism which lies behind it, revealing at the same time his
fundamental belief in the existence of natural law and in the
possibility of science. Holding this faith, the great Greek
naturalists, from Thales to Democritus, had boldly faced the
problem of the cosmos, and sought to wring from nature her
secret. To their work Thucydides supplied, so to speak, the
counterpart in history, and by exhibiting a world which was
ruined by the crime and folly, as it might have been saved by

[1] p. 136, above.   [2] *Later Roman Empire*, i. 311.

the virtue and intelligence of men, he offered a naturalistic interpretation of human life.

The revival in modern times of the scientific and historical spirit has been a slow process, although its beginnings can be traced to the period of the Renaissance. Of this spirit Machiavelli announced himself the herald when, in penning the preface to his *Discourses on Livy*,[1] he declared:

Albeit the jealous temper of mankind, ever more disposed to censure than to praise the works of others, has constantly made the pursuit of new methods and systems no less perilous than the search after unknown lands and seas; nevertheless, prompted by that desire which nature has implanted in me, fearlessly to undertake whatsoever I think offers a common benefit to all, *I enter a path which, being hitherto untrodden by any*,[2] though it involve me in trouble and fatigue, may yet earn me thanks from those who judge my efforts in a friendly spirit. And, although my feeble discernment, my slender experience of current affairs, and imperfect knowledge of ancient events, render these efforts of mine defective and of no great utility, they may at least open the way to some other, who, with better parts and sounder reasoning and judgement, shall carry out my design, whereby if I gain no credit, at all events I ought to incur no blame.

In these words Machiavelli proclaimed his belief that history is the real teacher of mankind, and threw out a hint of the future development of the historical principle. In subsequent passages he affirmed his faith in the uniformity of nature, apart from which, as we have said, the past is without significance for the present 'as though the heavens, the sun, the elements, and man himself were no longer the same as they formerly were as regards motion, order, and power'. This faith he affirms explicitly in several passages, of which we may note one, because it corresponds so remarkably with the views of Thucydides on the same subject.

The wise are wont to say, and not without reason, or at random, that he who would forecast what is about to happen should look to what has been; since all human events, whether present or to come, have their exact counterpart in the past. And this, *because these events are brought about by men, whose passions and dispositions*

[1] A.D. 1510. Eng. Transl., N. H. Thomson, 1883.
[2] The italics in this and the two following quotations are mine.

remaining in all ages the same naturally give rise to the same effects;
although doubtless, the operation of these causes takes a higher
form, now in one province and now in another, according to the
character of the training wherein the inhabitants of these provinces
acquire their way of life.[1]

In this passage we may note the significant rôle which
Machiavelli attributes to νόμος—the cultural and institutional
environment—in moulding the characters of men. In a subsequent paragraph (46) he further develops his views on this
subject:

> Manners and institutions differing in different cities, seem here
> to produce a harder and there a softer race ; and a like difference may
> also be discerned in the character of different families in the same
> city. . . . These qualities we cannot refer wholly to the *blood*, for
> that must change as a result of repeated intermarriages, but must
> ascribe rather to the different *training and education* given in different
> families. For much turns on whether a child of tender years hears
> a thing well or ill spoken of, since this must needs make an impression
> on him whereby his whole conduct in after life will be influenced. . . .

Commonplace as these words may now appear, their significance in the mouth of Machiavelli can hardly be exaggerated.
They serve indeed to bridge the gap of centuries, linking him
on the one hand with Thucydides and the Hippocratics, and
on the other with the sociologists of modern times. For they
indicate something which is vastly more significant than a mere
belief in history, and that is a perception of the methodological
principles involved if history is to be treated as a science. These
principles Machiavelli perceived as though by a flash of
inspiration, and it appears that he used them in his various
scientific studies of the French, Swiss, and German people, as
well as in his history of Florence. But for the rest, even
Machiavelli was content to take his 'history' as he found it,
and make (of all texts in ancient literature!) the first decade of
Livy the basis of his generalizations upon society and politics.

It was not any lack of interest in the past but rather defective
methodology which for so long retarded the development of
scientific history in modern times, and in effect left Machiavelli

[1] *Discourses,* iii. 43.

without a real successor at least until the time of Niebuhr's famous journey to Berlin (1810). In saying this, we do not wish to disparage the valuable work done by Renaissance and Reformation scholars, and particularly by the members of the Benedictine foundation at St. Maur, without whose indefatigable labours in collecting and criticizing the scattered texts, the achievement of the nineteenth century would have been impossible. But so far as concerns the standards of interpretation, one may judge of the condition of history, even at the close of the eighteenth century, by pausing to consider the work of Gibbon, who from his close resemblance to the Father of History might almost be called the Herodotus of modern times.

There is indeed more than a slight analogy between the historian of the Persian wars and the historian of the Decline and Fall. Each took as his theme the clash of civilization and barbarism, and by both a vast canvas was slowly worked up with strokes of unerring precision and power. Herodotus and Gibbon were each filled with a consuming intellectual curiosity, and this indeed seems in both cases to have been the motive impelling them through the dense forest through which their path lay; for they were both in a very real sense pioneers, and each set for his day and generation a standard of historical composition far superior to anything hitherto known. Both were creatures of an age of enlightenment, and both were rationalists, regarding themselves as emancipated from the conventional beliefs and inhibitions of their day. From the poets and philosophers Herodotus had drawn his belief in a vague Deity (ὁ θεός, τὸ θεῖον) which he had substituted in his own mind for the popular belief. For the Trinity of the Christian Church, Gibbon had substituted the Deism which had been postulated as a philosophic necessity by contemporary speculation. Both Herodotus and Gibbon, while professing contemptuous aloofness from the various conventional beliefs and practices which came under their observation, were none the less fascinated by those beliefs and practices, and made the most persistent effort to explain them away in terms of contemporary rationalism. Both also admitted metaphysical canons

best illustrated by the controversies which have arisen in connexion with the use of the term 'nature'. 'Nature' is a concept
which from the standpoint of scientific methodology has a
sufficiently definite meaning. As applied to man, it includes
the whole environment which creates him, and which he helps
to create, and which is therefore, as Hippocrates declared,
proper to his nature. Yet the Sophists, seizing upon the
sufficiently obvious distinction between the physical foundation
of all life and the man-made convention which is its super-
structure, made this distinction the basis of a criticism of the
existing social and political order, as though it were scientifically
legitimate to wrench man from his setting, and use the word
'nature' in two senses at one and the same time. Socrates
was less simple or less disingenuous. He boldly introduced
absolute ideas, and made them the touchstones of actuality;
but he never pretended that in doing so he was being other than
philosophic. Those who share his belief that criticism of man
and society is possible in terms other than those of welfare and
power should be no less frank than he. They should admit that
no such standards can be discovered within the limits of science,
but are really inspired by religion and philosophy.

INDEX